The Drinking Man's Guide
to the BVI
by
Julian Putley

Published by
Virgin Island Books
P.O. Box 8309 • Cruz Bay, St. John
US Virgin Islands 00831
e-mail: putley@sunfunbvi.com

Illustrations by Bob Nock

The Drinking Man's Guide to the BVI

The Drinking Man's Guide to the BVI now enters its third edition. Every year this little guide book finds more and more fans and is proof that the scholarly Ben Franklin was correct when he said: "Beer is proof that God loves us and wants us to be happy."

The Drinking Man's Guide is about FUN. In fact that's what a holiday in the BVI is all about. It's just so dazzlingly beautiful with great beach bars, nightspots and party venues around every corner. So while you're relaxing under the tropical sun, sailing away on a beautiful yacht to palm lined powdery beaches or waiting to dive into warm azure waters just peruse this guide and let the good times roll…cos fun is on the menu. It is often quoted that "if you can't have fun here, you can't have fun anywhere."

Nearly every evening of a Caribbean holiday will involve visiting a beach bar, club, or nightspot where reggae, calypso, blues or steel pan music will be playing. This guide shows you the best places to go with favorite drink recipes and special happenings.

The Caribbean has long been noted for its calypso songs; spontaneous topical commentary that usually concerns everyday life, family or political scandal in humorous ways, often with sexual nuance. The clever cartoons are by internationally renowned graphic artist Bob Nock. The short stories and limericks are by Julian Putley and are sure to bring a smile to the face of even the most world-weary.

A Note on the Free Offers and Giveaways

In keeping with the fun nature of this book most bars are offering free drinks and giveaways. Sebastian's, Neptune's Treasure and Myett's are giving away a free bottle of wine per table with dinner. Nearly every bar is giving away a free specialty drink, tropical cocktail or rum smoothie

In the back of the book are coupons. All you do is take the book with you to the bar and show them the coupon so that they can void it and then supply you with their special offer. DO NOT cut out the coupons, as they will then be valueless. Then keep the book as a souvenir of your pub-crawl around the BVI

Note: Not all bars are in this guide. In the BVI the rum shops are too numerous to include every one. Also restaurants with minimal bar facilities have other publications that fulfill their needs.

Jost Van Dyke

NOT TO BE USED FOR NAVIGATION

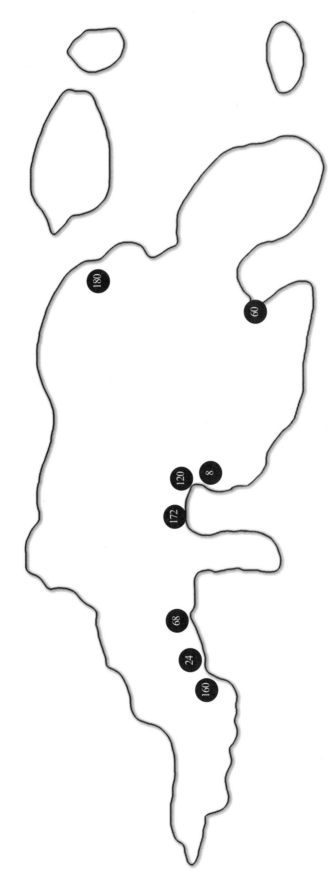

Tortola

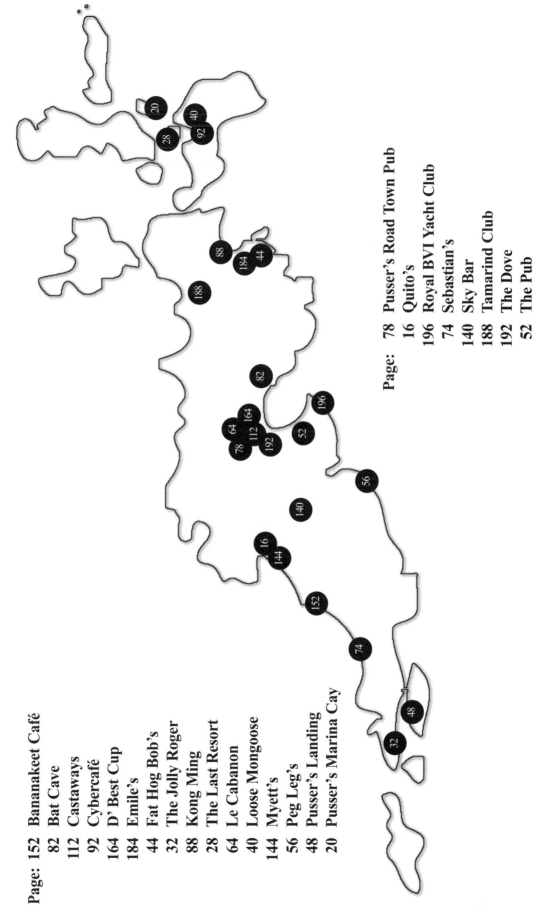

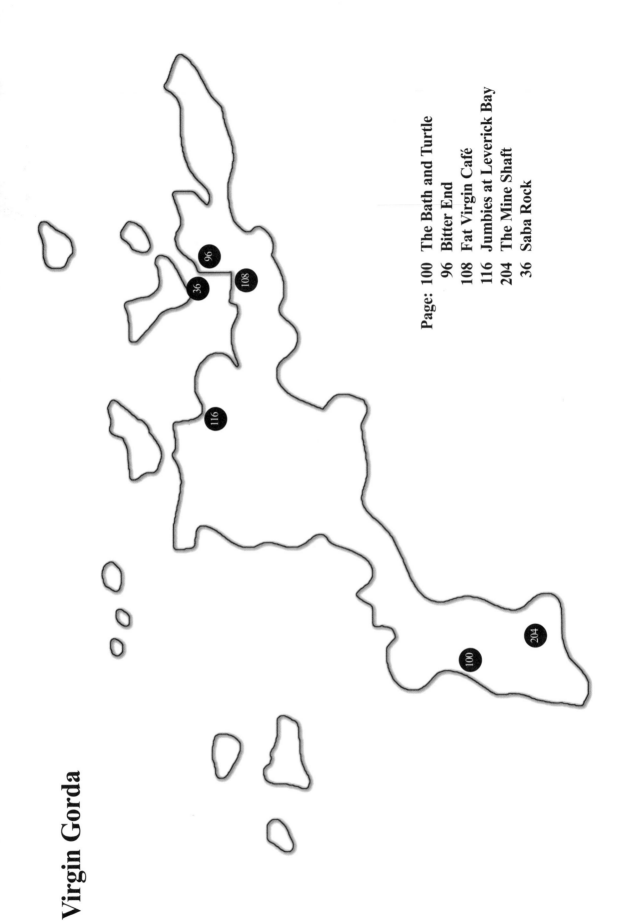

Virgin Gorda

Anegada

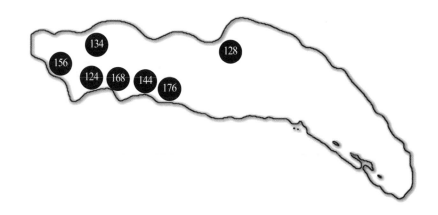

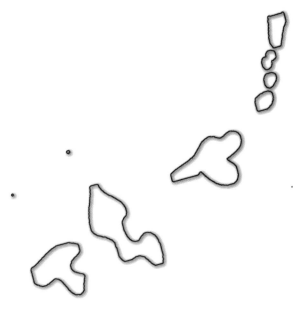

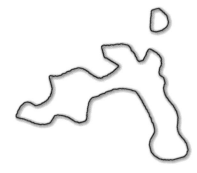

Norman Island

Foxy's

Giveaway coupon in back!

Foxy's

Twas a party night in town
New Year's had come around
The bay was packed
Then the wind, it backed
And boats just ran aground

The moon aligned with Mars
It outshone all the stars
Then late that night
Skies filled with light
From rockets fired from bars

Twas ol' year's night at Foxy's
The bar was full of hotties
The band played on
Till the sun, it shone
New year was here
To me twas clear
Foxy's just has no copies

Cryptic Comments

Politics is supposed to be the second oldest profession. In fact it bears a very close resemblance to the first.

Foxy's

Foxy's is, without a doubt, the most famous beach bar in the Virgin Islands, if not the entire Caribbean. It started from small beginnings in 1968 with a lean-to affair next to the church in Great Harbour on Jost van Dyke's south side, erected temporarily to supply refreshments for an island fete. After that Foxy's moved to its present location behind the palms at the eastern end of the bay but for years it was only a simple palm frond shack. In those early days there were no bareboats but crews and guests of large yachts needed a good watering hole with cold beer and quality rum, and Foxy's was there. Often it was a help yourself arrangement and Foxy would sometimes call in between fishing trips and tell a story or two. His magnetic personality endeared him to everyone.

In 1974 two sailors were drinking rum at the bar and arguing the merits of their two boats and when the arguing got to loud gesticulating it was Foxy who suggested a race: the first wooden boat race was born. The music at the party that night was a local scratch band with Ruben Chinnery playing lead and today he is still one of the islands' most popular entertainers. And there you have it, the recipe for success: tropical shack, laid back style, rum drinks and cold beer, a happy, story-telling host and great music.

Today the ambiance is not much different to what it was in those early days. There's a popular restaurant, a gift shop and the bar is festooned with mementos from thousands of visitors and years of parties: the 33rd annual wooden boat race has just concluded and the winners of the various categories will have their names carved into the prestigious name boards.

Now mega parties are organized at Christmas and Old Year's Night and sometimes the new stadium out back is used for private parties. One recent one for a fiftieth birthday party hired The Beach Boys, who flew down with a large entourage for the one night show. Yep, Foxy's has come a long way.

But the magic of Foxy's is that the old-time flavor has been retained while hundreds of visitors are welcomed, watered, fed and entertained daily. Foxy, barefoot, baggy pants and knotty dreads poking out from under a baseball cap will play an impromptu calypso that will be about the most topical event. He'll laugh at you…and then he'll laugh at himself…and then he'll laugh with you. Wife Tessa, not far in the background, will be choreographing the day's business activities and everything seems to roll along with so little effort that visitors go away shaking their heads in wonder.

In the words of one of the locals "It jus' a Jost van Dyke ting."

Specialty Drink

Dread Fox

Ingredients: 1 shot Foxy's Firewater rum

                   2 shots Silver Fox rum

                   2 ounces margarita mix

                   cranberry juice & a twist of fresh lime

Method: Pour over ice cubes, mix and finish with freshly grated nutmeg.

Willy T

Unique, casual dining on board on the water.
Open for Lunch and Dinner.
Late night parties and hot dancing music.
A fun time guaranteed!

Tel: 496-8603 • VHF: CH 16 • www.williamthornton.com

Willy T

There's a floating bar in the Bight
It's really quite out o' sight
It's not to be missed
It's on everyone's list
For the first, or perhaps the last night

You should try their famous 'ski shot'
The tequila's the best of the lot
After good grub
In that water-borne pub
You'll go back to your boat feeling hot

Girls love to be licked on the bar
For a moment they feel like a star
Called 'The Body Shot'
The lads like it a lot
The most fun for all…by far!

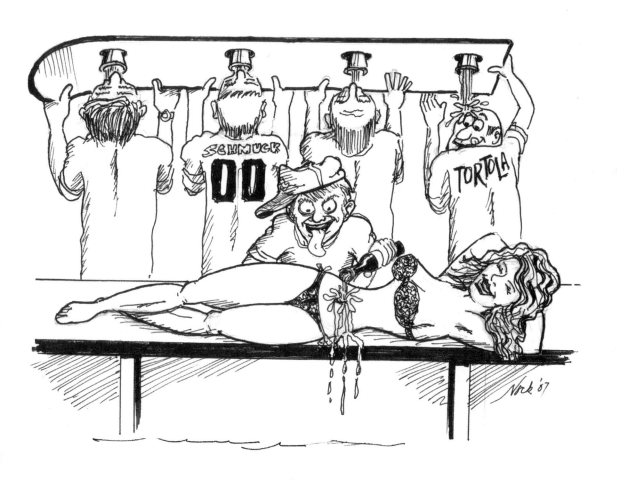

Cryptic Comments

Character, like tea, shows its strength in hot water.

Willy T

An old, wooden Baltic Trader that was no longer fit for service as a sailing vessel was found to be perfect as a restaurant, bar and party venue. The brainchild of Mick and Annie Gardner the old vessel was named after one of Tortola's most famous sons, Quaker, William Thornton. It was anchored in the southwest corner of Norman Island's Bight in 1989. The parties began. Whether it was the weight of continuous dancing partygoers or just plain old age the original Willy T gave up the ghost and sank in 1995. But by 1996 a new steel vessel had been found and was equipped with new generators, kitchen and bar equipment, and now you can scuba dive on the Willy T and dine on the Willy T all on the same day. (The old vessel was floated and re-sunk as a dive site off Great Harbor, Peter Island).

Famous for "grub and grog" with healthy portions of local fish and West Indian dishes at both lunch and dinner, the Willy T has also gained notoriety for outrageous and riotous happenings. Ski shots and revealing body shots in an atmosphere of party music, wild dancing and cavorting all make this particular watering hole a place that pirates of yesteryear would be proud of.

~~

Toast

To Honor! If you get honor. Stay on her.

Specialty Drink

<u>The Body Shot</u>

Ingredients: Sparsely clad body

1 shot tequila

1/2 teaspoon salt

wedge of lime

Method: Make sure body is as sparsely clad as is indecently possible. Body should lie face up on bar. Salt is sprinkled on neck of supplicant and then licked off by partner. Tequila is poured into belly button of supplicant and lapped up by partner (sometimes liquor dribbles off and into surrounding areas - this must be licked off since it is very bad luck to waste any). Wedge of lime is placed in supplicant's bikini bottoms or panties. Partner sucks juice out (of lime).

Note: These drinks are very more-ish.

Cryptic Comments

He who throws mud, loses ground.

Quito's Gazebo

Tortola's Hottest Nightspot
Quito and his Band The Edge Fridays and Saturdays
Quito solo most other nights
Intimate atmosphere. World Class Reggae.
Lunch and Dinner served daily.

Tel: 495-4837 • VHF: CH 16 • www.quitorymer.com

Giveaway coupon in back!

Quito's Gazebo

Visit Quito's, it's always a blast
The reggae's a blast from the past
It's time for a party
With look-alike Marley
Bob's in the superstar class

The 'Edge' is the name of the band
The best reggae band in the land
Rasta's they love it
Tourists aren't above it
Dance on the beach in the sand

So if you're feeling sad and alone
Get a taxi to Quito's from home
Or give him a call
Come on down, have a ball
Unless you're 'hotter on the phone'

Cryptic Comments

Never seen a miracle?
Just look at the dumb cow.
It can turn grass into milk.

Quito's Gazebo

Since the mid 80s Quito's has been the hottest nightspot in Tortola. Native son Quito Rhymer is a talented artist and musician as well as a successful businessman and most nights the club is thronging with a diverse group of partygoers and music fans. The Gazebo is right on the beach at beautiful Cane Garden Bay with a spectacular view over the water to Jost van Dyke. The stage is set back behind a small dance floor and on Friday and Saturday nights, giant speakers pump out the live reggae rhythms of Quito and his popular band "The Edge." On most other nights Quito will play solo in a somewhat more intimate atmosphere. In the early evening the restaurant on the veranda serves island style food with the emphasis on fish dishes.

Over the years Quito has become very popular locally and a plethora of CDs are testament to his skill as an imaginative and prolific entertainer. You can catch the real Caribbean island flavor here.

~~

Toast

May all your ups and downs be in bed.

Specialty Drink

Quito's Legend

Ingredients: 1 shot white Bacardi rum

1 shot Smirnoff vodka

1 shot peach schnapps

1 shot blue Curacao

1 ounce sweet and sour (sugar syrup and lime)

3 ounces 7-Up

1 ounce grenadine

Method: Pour into a 12 ounce glass over ice cubes the rum, vodka and peach schnapps. Slowly add blue Curacao and syrup. Carefully add the 7up and slowly pour in the grenadine. The final cocktail should have a layered look: orange, blue and pink. Garnish with an orange slice, lime slice and a maraschino cherry.

Cryptic Comments

A bird in the hand is the best way to eat chicken.

Marina Cay

Free Ferry from Beef Island
Wide selection of appetizers, main dishes and succulent desserts.
Rob White Bar on the Hill for Happy Hour Specials and Entertainment by popular musician "Beans".

Tel: 494-2174 • VHF: CH 16 • www.pussers.com

Marina Cay

There once was a pretty mermaid
She was topless and smiled all day
At Happy Aaaarhh
Now she's star of the bar
And that is the way it has stayed

Pusser's at Marina Cay
Is where everyone wants to be
When Beans is on stage
It is all the rage
The most fun, I guarantee

'Sailin' down to Soper's Hole'
The song inspires the sailor's goal
Of a downwind run
With Pusser's rum
Yeah! Pirates are in control!

Cryptic Comments

We do not see things as they are.
We see them as we are.

Marina Cay

The most popular rum in Tortola is Pusser's: a blend of five rums and the recommended ingredient of many cocktails, the most famous being the "Painkiller."

The term Pusser is derived from Purser, the man on board ship responsible for ship's stores, and for over 300 years the Royal Navy distributed a rum ration to the sailors: this ceased in 1970. In 1979, Charles Tobias, founder of Pusser's West Indies Ltd., obtained license from the Admiralty to blend the famous rum and soon it was being bottled in Tortola, where it is widely available today. Pusser's now has four bar/restaurants in the BVI and as many quality gift shops. The bar/restaurants are all in beautiful locations but none more so than Marina Cay.

In the late 30s Marina Cay was bought by romantic writer and novelist Rob White and his new wife Rodie for the princely sum of 60 pounds sterling. He built the small house on top of the island and the couple lived a sort of Robinson Crusoe lifestyle for several years while Rob wrote a book about the experience, "Two on the Isle," later made into a movie with Sidney Poitier and John Cassevetes

Today the little house on the hill has been restored and the patio is used for a happy hour bar where Pusser's Painkillers and ice cold beers are available while you enjoy the entertainment of Michael Beans; a consummate entertainer, one-man-band, and island character.

The food is excellent at the breezy beach restaurant and a free ferry leaves from Beef Island hourly.

Specialty Drink

Pusser's Painkiller

Ingredients: 2 shots Pusser's rum

1 ounce orange juice

4 ounces pineapple juice

1 ounce coconut cream (Coco Lopez)

Method: Mix all ingredients in a blender. Pour over ice and garnish with freshly grated nutmeg and a maraschino cherry

Cryptic Comments

Anything good in life is either illegal, immoral or fattening.

Soggy Dollar Bar

"Home of the Original Painkiller"
Great Beach Bar
Casual Lunches
Gourmet Candlelit Dinners

Phone: (284) 495-9888 • Fax (284) 495-9999
www.soggydollar.com • relax@soggydollar.com

Giveaway coupon in back!

Soggy Dollar Bar

The most famous beach bar in the land
Situated on powder white sand
Their famous Painkiller's
The Soggy bar's thriller
More often than not it's just crammed

For years they've been top of the list
It's a bar that's not to be missed
You could get groggy
Drinkin' at the Soggy
It's the price you pay, being pissed

At the Soggy leave a drink for your mates
If they're coming down from the States
They'll be sure to foller
If you leave a five dollar
A surprise at the Soggy awaits

Toast: (courtesy "Beans")

May the wind at your back not be your own.

Soggy Dollar Bar

The White Bay Sandcastle is the name of the little resort that incorporates the famous Soggy Dollar Bar. They are both little changed from the way they were in 1971 when George Myrick opened the now famous beach resort, except that the volume of traffic has increased a hundredfold; and by traffic I mean boat traffic. The sandy beach at White Bay rises steeply to the palm trees so the beach is visible from quite a distance, hence the name. The texture of the sand is particularly fine, almost powdery, and this is largely the result of a substantial fringing reef. Between beach and reef is crystal clear turquoise water about 8-ft deep and perfect for anchoring when there's no ground sea. Once anchored the beach is so inviting that many people jump in and swim straight to the beach and then walk on up to the bar – with wet money to buy drinks. Hey presto! The Soggy Dollar Bar. It's probably the only bar with a clothesline with wet dollars hanging out to dry.

The bar is very casual – people look at you askance if you're wearing shoes. Lounge chairs and hammocks are provided for patrons and if you succumb to more than one of their famous Painkillers you can try your skills at a variety of bar games and puzzles like the ring game, nail puzzle or Jenga. It's the perfect spot for a cheeseburger in paradise, but the more adventurous might try a flying fish sandwich. Reservations requested by 4 p.m. for their gourmet, four course, candlelit dinner in the open-air, beach front restaurant.

Specialty Drink

Painkiller

Ingredients: Pusser's Dark Rum

coconut cream (Coco Lopez)

orange juice

pineapple juice

Method: Mix all ingredients in a blender, pour over ice cubes and garnish with freshly grated nutmeg and a maraschino cherry.

Note: The Soggy Dollar Bar invented this drink and the exact proportions are kept secret. Experiment a little until you get the mixture you like.

Cryptic Comments

**A word to wives and girlfriends everywhere.
Men have two needs: food and sex.
So if he doesn't have an erection,
make him a sandwich.**

The Last Resort

Casual & Friendly Atmosphere.
Great Happy Hour with hors d'oeuvers menu
Dinner: fine selection of a la carte dishes
After Dinner Show with the Singing Chef &
House Band • Bohemian Style Gift Shop

Tel: 495-2520 • VHF: CH 16

In Trellis Bay there's a cay
Named for a rascal, Bellamy
He did plunder and pillage Every town and small village
Even burn, that mercenary

But peace now reigns on that isle
And the restaurant is quite island style
Even the deaf Love the Singing Chef
His performance will bring on a smile

The food isn't half bad
And the chef isn't all mad
He's got a good flunky Named Bottom the donkey
That ass is not a new fad

Often it gets kinda busy
Bottom runs around in a tizzy
A carrot here Then a drink of beer
He helps till everyone's dizzy

He's called a 'nice piece of ass'
Really nothing short of world class
But the Singing Chef Calls on the Ref
When Bottom lets go his gas.

Cryptic Comments

The real mystery of life is not a problem to be solved, it is a reality to be experienced.

The Last Resort

The Last Resort

The Last Resort has been around so long it's hard for anyone to remember when there wasn't a Last Resort. The popular restaurant, bar and cabaret venue moved to its present location on Bellamy Cay in Trellis Bay in 1973 having started operations on Little Jost van Dyke in '71. Proprietors Tony and Jackie Snell built up a thriving business with a "Gargantuan buffet" and a "Year's supply of belly laughs." Over the years the little island became home to a diverse collection of wounded birds, stray animals and other lost and lonely four-legged friends that big-hearted Jackie could not leave to the wiles of nature. Some of these became incorporated in the show and soon there was star billing for "Singing Dogs and a Performing Donkey." Many amusing stories derived from the animals: When the donkey named Chocolate died (from sclerosis of the liver, it is said) she was weighted down with a couple of defunct outboards and buried at sea. Now, occasionally, yachtsmen report seeing a donkey speeding between the islands leaving a large wake. Another donkey, Vanilla, after years and years as a superstar, absconded one full moon night, a bad mistake since donkey feet are small and not good for swimming. Unfortunately she drowned before making it ashore. Now "Bottom," a new very wise ass, is a rising star – but recently he disappeared. Perhaps he has joined Chocolate and they are racing between the islands.

The after dinner show which starts at 9:00 p.m. may include the "Singing Chef" with the Houseband or nightly guest artists.

Sadly, Jackie has passed on, and Tony is semi-retired but still makes an occasional guest appearance. New proprietors, daughter Jessica and Ben will ensure you have a warm welcome and an entertaining evening.

Specialty Drink

Island Moose

Ingredients: 2 shots Mount Gay amber rum

                      2 ounces Baileys coffee liqueur

                      2 ounces coconut cream (Coco Lopez)

                      1 shot Kahlua

Method: Blend all the ingredients and serve over ice.

                      Garnish with freshly grated nutmeg and a maraschino cherry.

Cryptic Comments

Money is the root of all wealth.

Atheism is a non-prophet organization.

The Jolly Roger

Great Food
Party Atmosphere on the Waterfront
Live music most weekends
Rooms available

Tel: 495-4559 • VHF: CH 16 • www.jollyrogerbvi.com

The Jolly Roger

It's the name of the pirates' flag
Innocent sailors would gag
You'd hear loud moans
The Skull and Cross Bones
Was a terrible, fearsome rag

They'd board you and steal the ship
Sail it away at a clip
Tear all asunder
Pillage and plunder
Put an end to your sailing trip

The Queen would have them flogged
If their position was properly logged
But the pub called the Jolly Roger
Was where they'd become a lodger
Then the 151
Would have 'em done
Instead of being flogged they'd be grogged

Cryptic Comments

Forgive your enemies:
it messes with their heads.

The Jolly Roger

In the early 80s some questionable piratical types started a small bar on the site that now houses the famous Jolly Roger Inn, which came into being in 1986. It started out catering to mariners and has retained that image to this day, now being host to the West End Yacht Club. It is renowned for riotous revelry and unforgettable parties with internationally famous bands such as Dick Solberg and the Sun Mountain Band and the legendary Tony O' Blues Band. The most famous race sponsored by The JR is the Sweethearts of the Caribbean, a race involving classic wooden yachts.

The Inn's restaurant serves delicious meals with a West Indian flair at reasonable prices. Rooms are available. The bar is usually a hive of activity and is patronized by locals and tourists alike.

~

Toast

Here's to the deep blue sea with no land in sight. Emerald Isles, fine wine and the lass that stays all night. (M. Beans)

Specialty Drink

<u>Jolly Roger Rum Punch</u>

Ingredients: 1 shot light rum

1 shot dark rum

equal parts guava

orange and pineapple juice

1 ounce grenadine

1 shot Myers dark rum

Method: Reserve the Myers. Mix all other ingredients together and pour over ice. Float the Myers on top and finish with grated fresh nutmeg. Garnish with a slice of orange and a maraschino cherry.

If you don't feel jolly after a couple of these you never will!

Cryptic Comments

Raising teenagers is like trying to nail Jello to a tree.

Saba Rock

Fine waterfront dining
Over the water bar • Shipwreck jewelry
Buffet $29.95
Special room rates for boaters
NEW!! Underwater light show!! See the fish!!

www.sabarock.com

Saba Rock

The island that's known as 'The Rock'
Is sometimes a bit of a shock
That giant meal
Just can't be real
But a graphic by artist, Bob Nock

The food is really superb
A buffet, described in their blurb
On their web cam
Eating all you can
Avoid at all costs a loud burp!!

There's a 'special' on the price of a room
Your girlfriend will want one quite soon
"I'm off that ol' boat
It's barely afloat,
And I'm really not feeling in tune."

Toast

There'll be no friggin' in the riggin' till the friggin' riggin' has been rigged for friggin' in

Saba Rock

Saba Rock is today famous for its "All You Can Eat" buffet dinners in an open-air bar/restaurant that overlooks Virgin Gorda's beautiful North Sound. It also offers an underwater museum in the form of an aquarium and an impressive system of underwater lights has been installed to highlight the literally hundreds of fish that swim, frolic and feed just below the deck.

Many people still talk of the way Saba Rock used to be as "The Pirate's Pub." It developed quite by accident when internationally renowned scuba diver, Bert Kilbride, moved his residence and dive operation there in the 1980s. When the dive operation was sold, seventy something Bert with his new wife, thirty something Gayla continued to live there but were continuously bothered by intrusive tourists. One day Bert threw his hands in the air in despair and decided to open a small bar and restaurant. "If you can't beat 'em join 'em" and "The Pirate's Pub" was born. It was a simple affair but had tons of character with palm frond roofs, rickety deck; and a waterfall, fishpond and a couple of parrots in the bar. In David Thrasher's "Bars of the BVI," published in 1992, the bar featured on the front cover.

"The Rock" is still considered the party venue of North Sound with all kinds of special offers for visiting yachtsmen. Free water and ice are offered to those who tie up to a Saba Rock mooring ball. The museum that holds cannons and an anchor from the famous RMS *Rhone* is an interesting aside and the gift shop houses nautical artifacts and sells authentic wreck jewelry.

Specialty Drink

<u>**Mai Tai**</u>

Ingredients: 2 shots white rum

1 shot Curacao

1 ounce sweet and sour mix (sugar syrup and lime juice)

2 ounces pineapple juice

1shot dark Myers rum

Method: Reserve the Myers rum. Mix all other ingredients together in shaker with ice. Pour over ice cubes and finish with a float of the Myers rum. Garnish with a wedge of lime and a maraschino cherry.

Cryptic Comments

George Bush:
"Ten out of ten people surveyed on the street were pedestrians"!

The Beef Island Guest House
& de Loose Mongoose
Restaurant

Loose Mongoose

Casual, friendly beach bar & restaurant
Breakfast • Lunch • Dinner
Sunday Night Live Music and BBQ
Rooms available

Tel: 495-2303 • VHF: CH 16 • mongoose@surfbvi.com
www.beefislandguesthouse.com

Giveaway coupon in back!

Loose Mongoose

A rodent is out on the loose
He's sexy and loose as a goose
He just doesn't care
He'll take you to his lair
He's known as the Loose Mongoose

There's a beach bar in Trellis Bay
It's named for that rodent at play
The Loose Mongoose
Sells powerful juice
Have you romancin' all day

So that rodent is not all to blame
That bar'll have you joining the game
Their excellent rum
Will make you come…
Back for more of the same

Cryptic Comments

Life is not about how fast you run, or how high you climb, but how well you bounce.

The Beef Island Guest House
& de Loose Mongoose
Restaurant

Loose Mongoose

The Loose Mongoose in Trellis Bay opened its doors in 1982. It is one of the oldest bars in the Trellis Bay area and it started quite by accident. The kitchen and bar was originally the storeroom for the building materials for the Beef Island Guest House. When the guesthouse was finished a few minor alterations to the shed metamorphosed it into a small bar and restaurant and today it is a popular stopover for visitors and locals alike. Situated right on the sheltered sandy beach with lounge chairs, hammocks and picnic tables under the palms the location is perfect for a frosty, happy hour drink.

An unusual beach game played here is horseshoes and on Sunday evenings there's a barbecue cooked under the beach gazebo followed by live music.

~~

Toast

Here's to the bones of Silas McVay, who died while defending his right of way. He was right, dead right, as he sailed along, but he's just as dead as if he were wrong.

Specialty Drink

Mongoose Magic

Ingredients: 2 shots of 151 amber Cruzan rum

1 shot Kahlua

1 ounce cream of coconut (Coco Lopez)

1/2 cup pineapple juice

Method: Blend ingredients with half-cup crushed ice.

No-See-Um

Ingredients: 2 shots of 151 amber Cruzan rum

1 ounce cream of coconut (Coco Lopez)

1/2 cup fruit punch and pineapple juice

1/2 banana

Method: Blend ingredients with half cup crushed ice.

Cryptic Comments

Hard work never killed anyone, but why take chances.

Fat Hog Bob's

Breezy waterfront restaurant at Hodges Creek
Hog-sized Portions – specializing in BBQ ribs,
chicken, steak, lobster and fish
"Best Burgers" - by the Daily News Survey
Hog sized breakfasts served daily. Takeout avail.

Tel: 495-1010 • VHF: CH 16

Fat Hog Bob's

If you feel like a really big steak
It's a sixty eight ounce that they make
Four pounds of meat
Could last you a week
All at once it could keep you awake

Some they come for the ribs
Their sauce is the best, no fibs
The meat you'll be pickin'
Your fingers a lickin'
Don't be a quibblin'
'bout sauce that be dribblin'
At Bob's they supply you with bibs

Toast

Here's to wherever you travel, near or faaaar…remember God loves ya…just the way y'aaaar. (M. Beans)

Fat Hog Bob's

Fat Hog Bob's opened its doors in January of 2000. Being one of the newest bars and restaurants in the territory, it has achieved amazing popularity in such a short time. The restaurant is renowned for its hog-size portions of steak, chicken, fish, ribs and lobster which are all grilled to perfection on the barbeque. They even have the best burgers in the Virgin Islands according to a "Daily News" survey of both US and British Virgin Islands residents and dare customers to eat their 48 oz steak (unassisted) by engraving their name on a plaque of "Hog Heroes", mounted proudly at the entrance, along with a 10% lifetime discount card for achieving this gluttonous feat.

The concept and design is credited to Bob Nock, a retired creative director and advertising agency owner, who sailed here fourteen years ago on his yacht and has never looked back. Clyde Chalwell, the owner, is a young entrepreneur from the BVI who maintains the daily operations of the restaurant and brings to life Bob's many creative ideas and special features that make Fat Hog Bob's unique. The ambience is tranquil, the ocean breeze refreshing and the view of the Sir Francis Drake Channel form the long deck is enchanting.

You can enjoy live music on Friday nights in season.

Specialty Drink

The Hogwacker

Ingredients: 1 shot amber rum

1 shot Stolichnaya vodka

1 shot Amaretto

1 shot Kahlua

1 shot Baileys and 2 ounces coconut cream (Coco Lopez)

Method: Mix all ingredients in a blender and pour over ice cubes. Garnish with a maraschino cherry. "Sealed with a kiss."

Cryptic Comments

A closed mouth gathers no foot.

Pusser's Landing

**On-the-water terrace and bar ~ Casual food
Rotis, burgers, pizzas, fish and chips,
sandwiches & more
Upstairs: fine dining overlooking the marina
Great wrap-around bar**

Tel: 495-4554 • VHF: CH 16 • www.pussers.com

Giveaway coupon in back!

Pusser's Landing

Down at the island's West End
You'll soon be on the mend
This Pusser's bar
Is for ol' Jack Tar
And his mates, sailors well hardened

Soper's Hole is a retreat
For sailors tired of the beat
The waitress is kind
So here they unwind
And hope for a moll… what a treat!

Some are escaping the noose
Their morals being loose as a goose
Perhaps they'd hang
Or join the chain gang
Not much between 'em to choose

Cryptic Comments

If you don't get everything you want, think of the things that you don't get that you don't want.

Pusser's Landing

Pusser's Landing is right on the water at the charming marina on the Frenchman's Cay side of Soper's Hole. Sailors can tie their dinghies at the restaurant's dock and step straight up to the bar and restaurant, which are adjacent to the boardwalk. Tables and chairs with shade umbrellas are attractively arranged in the Mediterranean style. In the evening dinner is served upstairs in a more formal setting.

All the usual delicious Pusser's rum cocktails are available, including the famous Painkiller, along with a formidable menu of tasty sandwiches, burgers, fish and chips and pizza, to name a few. This is a great place to relax and watch the yachts in the large and picturesque anchorage of Soper's Hole, once a pirates' den of iniquity.

~

Toast

**To the heat.
Not the heat that ignites and burns down shanties,
but the heat that excites and brings down panties.**

Specialty Drink

Sea Breeze

Ingredients: 1 shot of vodka

2 ounces cranberry juice

2 ounces grapefruit juice

Method: Mix all the ingredients and pour into a Collins glass.

Garnish with a slice of orange and a cherry. Very refreshing.

Marina Champagne

Ingredients: Champagne and mango syrup

Method: Pour into an 8 ounce glass half and half mango juice and champagne.

A fizzy tropical wonder. Enjoy.

Cryptic Comments

No-one is listening...until you fart.

The Pub

Tortola's Original English Pub
Great views of Road Town Harbour
whilst dining on a breezy veranda
Open for lunch & dinner • Internet service available

Tel: 494-2608 • VHF: CH 16 • www.thepubbvi.com

Giveaway coupon in back!

The Pub

The Pub is right on the water
Take your son, your mum or your daughter
It was the first
To quench your thirst
You remember it don't ya, ya ought ta

The pub goes back quite a while
Traditional food is their style
Not bangers and mash
Or corned beef hash
But Goat Water, I'd walk a mile

Chef Princess will feed ya till full
With food from the foot of a bull
Or perhaps pig tail
Washed down with light ale
Your taste buds will all be a tremble

Cryptic Comments

The winds of the world are always blowing, but you must set the sails.

The Pub

The Pub

The Pub is little changed from the way it was 39 years ago. Back then, in 1968, it was the first waterfront pub in the islands. Located by the island's lone small marina and adjacent to Road Town's anchorage it was the hub of the island's social life. You could get a plate of food, a pint of draught ale, and a game of darts, all in the good old British tradition.

Now there are marinas and bars everywhere but The Pub has remained a popular eatery and watering hole. MJ Blues plays weekly. There's an extensive veranda where you can eat and drink in cool comfort and watch the yachts at anchor and sometimes there's a band at weekends where you can dance on a courtyard type dance floor.

An annual event in August (around the 18th) that is a lot of fun is the self explanatory "Anything that floats but a boat race." It's a day of revelry, fun events and quite a bit of drinking. The sinking boat race is a highlight of the day where competitors have to navigate around a course in a sinking dinghy before it goes under.

Specialty Drink

Pub Daiquiri

Ingredients: 2 shots amber rum

1 ripe banana

1 ounce strawberry juice

1 ounce mango juice

2 ounces coconut cream (Coco Lopez)

1 cup crushed ice

Method: Pour all the ingredients into a blender with the crushed ice.
Blend thoroughly. Garnish with a maraschino cherry.

Cryptic Comments

Cannibals don't eat clowns: they taste funny.

What did the cannibal do after he dumped his girlfriend? He wiped his bottom.

Peg Leg's Landing

"Best Happy Hour on Tortola" from 5-7pm
Great Casual Dining in a Beautiful Setting

Tel: 494-0028 • VHF: CH 16 • www.nannycay.com

Giveaway coupon in back!

Peg Leg's Landing

T'is a pirate bar so I'm told
A pirate stronghold of old
It's in the lee
Of Nanny Cay
And the beer's guaranteed to be cold

If you lost your leg in a fight
Or a bullet took out half your sight
You'd be in good standing
At Peg Leg's Landing
Pirates can drink here all night

If you forgot to bring with you your gold
Left it stashed away in the hold
An IOU
Will probably do
Order a round, be bold!

Cryptic Comments

Sometimes I wake up grumpy; other times I let him sleep

Peg Leg's Landing

Nanny Cay is fast becoming the BVIs' most important marine centre and located on its southernmost tip is Peg Leg's Landing, a quality bar and restaurant, that enjoys cool trade wind breezes and a view overlooking the Sir Francis Drake Channel. It began life in 1987 when it became clear that the area needed a good hostelry. The two story wooden building with bar and restaurant on the second floor looks almost like a wild-west saloon with nooks and crannies everywhere.

There is a happy hour with drink specials and free bar snacks, and a popular and reasonably priced restaurant. During the day patrons can relax on a recliner by the pool or volleyball court while enjoying a frosty beer and a burger.

Many annual events have chosen Peg Leg's as their venue because of its extensive grounds and central location. In 2007 it was host to The BVI Spring Regatta and Gaming Night (a charitable event to support the animal shelter). People often choose the site for weddings and birthday parties too.

Specialty Drink

Peg Leg's Bushwacker

Ingredients: 1 shot Malibu coconut rum

1 shot Baileys

1 shot Kahlua

1 shot Amaretto

1 shot vodka

2 spoonfuls Hershey's chocolate syrup

Method: This recipe will make two drinks. Blend all ingredients with one cup of crushed ice. Garnish with a maraschino cherry.

Cryptic Comments

How do we solve the problem of the world's rising oceans? Ans: Grow more sponges.

Sidney's
Peace and Love

Honor bar
Monday & Saturday "Pig Roast!"
Thursday "All you can eat lobster & Live Band!"
Other Nights "Giant B-B-Q"
Help Yourself Bar!!

TEL: 495-9271 • VHF: CH 16

Giveaway coupon in back!

Sidney's Peace and Love

Sydney's is known for its cookin'
Give them a call and book in
Its home made style
Is the best by a mile
And the girls are really good lookin'

The ribs are real finger lickin'
And the rice to your ribs will be stickin'
The creamy cole slaw
Will have you callin' for more
Then dance with the girls, yeah! High kickin'

They have an island gift shop
It's a place where you just have to stop
While singing a song
Try on a sarong
Then return to the bar for a drop

Cryptic Comments

If con is the opposite of pro, what's the opposite of progress?

Sidney's Peace and Love

Tucked in behind the southwestern corner of Jost van Dyke's Little Harbor, in Careening Hole, Sidney's has been catering to the yachting crowd since 1982. Sidney is ably assisted by his wife, Adina, who does the cooking and two daughters who serve the meals and run the flamboyant gift shop. The establishment is truly a family run affair with an extremely friendly atmosphere. Before you even reach the dock one of the daughters, Strawberry or Janet, will be waiting to tie up your dinghy and as soon as you step ashore you are invited to the bar to mix your own drink, on the honor system. Meals are all local Caribbean fare with healthy portions. Sidney is a fisherman so lobster conch and fish are nightly features and accompaniments include fried plantain, Cole slaw, potato salad, corn, rice and beans. Chicken and ribs are usually available as well.

As you can imagine a help-yourself bar can get pretty rowdy at times and often visitors are tempted to leave their T-shirts behind, scrawled with an appropriate message of peace and love, of course. Now there are literally hundreds of T-shirts hanging from the ceiling.

Specialty Drink

You name it, cos you're going to mix it

Ingredients: Dark rum

light rum

more rum

then some more rum

Method: Pour over ice with a twist of lime. Sit down before drinking.

Cryptic Comments

Learn from your parents' mistakes, use birth control.

Le Cabanon

Fine French cuisine in an open air setting
Open for lunch and dinner
Bar open late
Great party atmosphere

Tel:494-8660

Le Cabanon

Look out, the froggies are comin'
With piano, guitar and some drummin'
They party at night
And do it up right
Till the wee hours it's a hummin'

Many have only one leg
Instead they have a wood peg
That froggy meat
Some like it to eat
Me, I'd rather just beg.

That froggy band can get rockin'
The crowd they often just flock in
Pate de foie?
Oui, c'est pour moi
But frog legs my throat will be blockin'

Cryptic Comments

I didn't fight my way to the top of the food chain to be a vegetarian.

Le Cabanon

Le Cabanon is in the heart of Road Town and concentrates on providing quality French cuisine in a quiet open-air atmosphere. The small bar is adjacent to the "boules" ground. Every summer a tournament is played and the winners of this classic French game, rather like the English "bowles," might well indulge in the famous specialty drink: The Cabanon Shot.

Owner/operator Christophe Boisgirard has built up a good reputation since opening in 1999; French ingredients are flown in weekly.

Sometimes the bar stays open late for special events and parties. The 2007 rugby world cup was well attended with an excited crowd drinking and eating while watching games on a large screen T.V.

~

Cryptic Comments

I love defenseless animals, especially in a good gravy.

Specialty Drink

The Cabanon Shot

Ingredients: 1 shot 151 proof rum

1 shot Jagermeister

2 ounces Red Bull

Method: Pour all ingredients into 4 ounce glass. Toss it back and order another one!!

Cryptic Comments

Whose cruel idea was it for the word lisp to have an 'S' in it?

Ivan's Local Flavor

Ivan's Local Flavor

Thursday Island BBQ,
Live Music with Ruben and his 12-string guitar
Island Menu • Ever Changing
All Star International Band.
Spontaneous Music. Come and join the fun.
Reservations Requested Tel: 495-9358 • VHF: CH 16
Moorings available. e mail: cupid1002@hotmail.com

Giveaway coupon in back!

Ivan's Honor Bar

Ivan's is right on the beach
It's really within easy reach
You know what they say
About Jost's White Bay
Of all the bays it's the peach

Ivan's has a great Thursday night
Their Barbecue is out o' sight
A 'stress free punch'
Is essential at lunch
Then you'll fly, high as a kite

Come and hear Ruben sing
At the Thursday night barbecue fling
Ruben will play
Requests all day
Among island musicians he's king.

Cryptic Comments

Eat right, exercise, die anyway.

Ivan's Local Flavor

Located on the sandy beach toward the east end of White Bay, Ivan's originated to serve campers in his campground adjacent to the bar. It soon became popular with the boating crowd because of its laid-back style, hammocks, honor bar and reasonably priced barbecue meals served on some evenings. Fresh fish is often on offer: Ivan is a fisherman in his rare moments of spare time.

It is a beach bar in the truest sense of the word: both interior and exterior are decorated with seashells in attractive designs and photographs of happenings and parties throughout the years and are displayed for all to see. On Thursdays during the season Ruben Chinnery sings from a huge repertoire of island classics accompanied by his twelve-string guitar. Locals and visiting musicians often join in and an impromptu scratch band or jam session is not uncommon. Many famous personalities and musicians have found Ivan's including Kenny Chesney, Keith Richard of the Rolling Stones, Dick Solberg and Willie Nelson. Some join the Ever Changing All Star International Band for an evening and make for an unforgettable time.

White Bay is a beautiful anchorage with crystal clear water and powdery sand but watch out for a ground sea if overnight anchoring is planned.

Specialty Drink

Ivan's Stress Free Punch

Ingredients: 2 teaspoons jelly from a female conch

1/2 cup water from a dildo cactus

Purée from one silly cybin mushroom

1/2 teaspoon of dried and powdered Billy goat scrotum

Finely diced bud of leatherback turtle

Method: Mix all ingredients in a blender.

Pour over ice and garnish with grated iguana tail.

Note: It has been said that this unusual cocktail will put lead in your pencil. It will also aid in finding a place to put your pencil.

Cryptic Comments

Some people are only alive because it's illegal to shoot them.

Wok the Dog

In the course of a lifetime there are sometimes moments when wonderful and terrible happenings occur simultaneously. Such was the case with Anna Nicole Smith when the death of a son and the birth of a daughter happened within days of each other. Friends of Charlie's, live-aboard cruisers turned charter yacht operators in the Virgin Islands had something similar happen to them:

Brian and Margaret's son Joe hadn't been back to see his parents for over three years. At med. school in the States he worked hard at his studies and during time off he worked in a bar to help pay his considerable expenses. Brian and Margaret were nearly always broke but one day they received a substantial deposit and sent five hundred bucks up to Joe to help pay for a visit. Soon it was all arranged and the happy parents were overjoyed, "We'll pick you up at the airport. We'll prepare your favourite Chinese food, you can have the aft cabin, we'll get the kayak ready."

The big day arrived and – big anti-climax – the couples little dog, Alpo, died. He'd been a crew member for twelve years, now there he was, belly up on the cabin sole. Margaret cried her eyes out and Brian couldn't console her. After another half hour they knew they would be late for their rendez-vous at the airport – what to do? They'd have a little burial ceremony tomorrow. Brian got a plastic bag and placed Alpo in it and put him in the fridge. They left for the airport.

They were almost an hour late. They searched high and low for Joe but couldn't find him. Then someone said he'd caught a cab. Brian and Margaret were dismayed. They couldn't believe how things were turning out.

Joe was a little disappointed but he knew life in the islands. The taxi drove him to the bay, he got a ride out to the family boat and threw his stuff below. He went straight to the fridge for a cold beer and – saw the dog!

Alpo was lying next to the Chinese noodles and the sweet and sour sauce. Joe's mind was racing. He'd heard of 'killing the fatted calf' but this was ridiculous.

Finally Brian and Margaret arrived back from the airport and there was much hugging and kissing, the chatter gushing. "You must be starving," said Margaret, "I'll get dinner going."

Joe was absolutely famished, "Actually, I'm not hungry at all," he lied, he couldn't get Alpo out of his mind. Then Brian produced a grocery bag with two crispy, golden brown ducks inside. Joe sighed with relief and relayed his fears to his Ma and Pa. They all laughed, "I really thought you were going to wok the dog," said Joe.

They uncorked a chilled bottle of white wine and made two toasts: one to a happy reunion and one to a safe journey for Alpo – to doggy heaven. They buried him next day.

~~

Cryptic Comments

Parents:
You spend the first two years of your children's life trying to get them to walk and talk and the next sixteen telling them to sit down and shut up.

Sebastian's on the Beach

Breakfast, Lunch, Sundowners and Dinner
Caribbean Flair with Flavour
Open: 8 am -10 pm Daily
Try our Famous 'Sebastian's Rum'

Tel: 495 4212 • www.sebastiansbvi.com

Giveaway coupon in back!

Sebastian's on the Beach

The Caribbean's the place for a rest
And the BVI is one of the best
Sebastian's by Sea
I'm sure you'll agree
Has the sand, the sea and the zest

Sebastian's is near to the cove
Where smugglers drop off their load
"Well done, my beauty
You got away payin' duty"
Then into the water he dove

Then grog he drank in large measure
Bragged about all of his treasure
While at "The Shack"
The law did attack
Now he's serving at the Queen's pleasure

Cryptic Comments

Worrying about something that may never happen is like paying interest on money you may never borrow.

Sebastian's on the Beach

Sebastian's is located on a luxurious, white sand beach in Little Apple Bay on Tortola's North Shore. For yachtsmen Sebastian's is easily accessible from Soper's Hole or Cane Garden Bay and makes an ideal stop for dinner and drinks for those wishing to enjoy Bomba's Shack on full moon nights.

On weekends, at the popular beach bar, you can dance under the stars to the live music of the islands' best fungi & steel bands.

For those seeking a memorable shore-side vacation, or perhaps a few days R and R after a sailing holiday, the charming 26 room hotel offers the ultimate in breathtaking scenery and total relaxation. At this casual, intimate hideaway, you can wake up to the sound of gently lapping waves and cool sea breezes. From the private balconies or terraces of our deluxe beachfront accommodations, enjoy spectacular views and colorful sunsets, or choose from one of the cheerfully appointed tropical garden rooms. Whatever your choice, the warm and friendly staff will make you feel at home.

The lunch menu features a wide variety of Caribbean rotis, hot and cold sandwiches, salads, burgers, homemade soups, wings and more.

For dinner you can choose from a variety of fish dishes, steaks, jerk chicken and fresh lobster in lime butter – to mention just a few choices.

Served on the palm-lined patio at the water's edge you can enjoy a taste of paradise here.

Specialty Drink

Rum Punch

Ingredients: 2 shots Sebastian's rum

                Equal parts: Orange juice

                Guava juice

                Pineapple juice

                Dash of Grenadine.

Method: Shake all ingredients in a cocktail shaker with ice. Pour over ice cubes and garnish with a sprinkling of grated nutmeg. Decorate with a slice of orange and a cherry. *Refreshing!*

Cryptic Comments

Always yield to temptation
because it may not come your way again.

It is easier to get forgiveness than permission.

Pusser's
Road Town Pub

Legendary Nautical Pub
Air Conditioned
Tortola's Best Happy Hour
Friday 2 for 1 drinks from 6-8 p.m.

Tel: 494-3897 • www.pussers.com

Giveaway coupon in back!

Pusser's Road Town Pub

This is a real sailors' pub
With large plates of good grub
If you're in good cheer
It's because of their beer
They serve it in a pint mug

Nelson would have swallowed a tot
Then planned his next froggy plot
It'd start as a probe
Then all over the globe
He'd chase them, that sorry lot

Victory meant 'splice the main brace'
Pour Pusser's rum in your face
If that grog
Put your brain in a fog
Have another and become an ace

Cryptic Comments

Going to church doesn't make you a Christian any more than going to a garage makes you a mechanic.

Pusser's Road Town Pub

Pusser's Pub originated in 1980 as a small bar on Road Town's waterfront near the ferry dock and was mainly an outlet for drinks made from the famous Pusser's rum, the Royal Navy's noggin for over 300 years. The Royal Navy's purser issued a daily rum ration to seamen on board ships from the year1666 to 1970 when the tradition was stopped. Entrepreneur and world-girdling sailor, Charles Tobias, acquired the rights to produce the fine, blended rum and he set up business in Tortola, BVI.

The present day Pusser's Pub opened in 1986 and has been a firm favourite with visitors and tourists ever since. The bar's Victorian ambiance is enhanced with waxed hardwood furniture, polished brass and subdued lighting, not unlike a good English pub…and it's air conditioned! The nautical theme is portrayed with antiques, mementoes and pictures depicting the Royal Navy's illustrious history as the greatest maritime nation in the world.

The menu is described as Caribbean and English pub fare. There are things like shepherd's pie, steak and kidney pie and pizzas. There are "Special Nights" too: Friday night is "2 for 1" on all drinks from 5 pm till 8pm. There's "Lady's Night" on Tuesdays and "Nickel Beer Night" on Thursdays.

There are several specialty drinks at Pusser's. "Nelson's Blood" has an interesting story behind it. When Nelson, hero of all England, was killed at the Battle of Trafalgar where he defeated the combined fleets of France and Spain his body was supposedly transported back to England in a casket of Pusser's rum. On the journey home some Jack Tars bored a hole in the casket and drank the rum. Hence Nelson's Blood.

Specialty Drink

The Painkiller Shooter, The Drink with the "Happy Ending"

Method: Into a tall shooter glass, pour 1-1/2 ozs Pusser's Rum. Add cold Painkiller Mix to the top, and watch the heavy, delicious mix go straight to the bottom. There it sits ready to provide a "Happy Ending" to all those finishing this awesome cocktail!

The Naked Lorna

This unique cocktail is one naked of all excess calories, except those found in its Pusser's rum.

Ingredients: Pusser's rum
                 lime juice
                 soda water
                 dash of Angostura bitters
                 dash of Stevia

Method.   Mix all ingredients in a cocktail shaker and pour over ice cubes. Garnish with a generous slice of lime.

Note: The drink's delightful balanced sweetness comes from a Peruvian plant called Stevia. It is a powerful anti-oxidant and thus Naked Lorna is good for you...God bless her!

The Bat Cave

**Great location at Baugher's Bay.
Still the swingingest bar and nighttime
party venue in Road Town**

Tel: 494-4880
www.spaghettijunction.net

Giveaway coupon in back!

Spaghetti Junction and the Bat Cave

If you feel like a plate of Italian
Have an appetite like that of a stallion
Head down to the Junction
And if there's no function
Eat enough for an army battalion

Then it's into the cave for a rave
Just right for a cute party slave
You'll feel all right
After dancing all night
And lovin' that babe that you crave

The music is always so hot
There are party lovers…a lot
"Hey, Mr DJ
Put on a replay
Of some of those mixes you've got!!"

Cryptic Comments

If you must choose between two evils, pick the one you've never tried before.

 # The Bat Cave

The Bat Cave is the swingingest bar and nighttime party venue in Road Town. The Bat Cave is housed in a grand location at Baugher's Bay in Road Town's east end. The best Italian food on the island is now served in spacious opulence and The Bat Cave still provides the best rave in town. At weekends the music and party atmosphere often go on into the wee hours, especially if there's a theme night. These nights might comprise a toga party, pajama party, punk party, pirate night or jazz special, to name but a few.

The Bat Cave developed from a restaurant called Spaghetti Junction that was originally located in the heart of Road Town. The restaurant was upstairs and the Bat Cave, on the lower level, came into being to meet a demand for a nightspot in town. In the year 2000 the location was changed to a venue at the east end of Inner Harbor Marina. Now, after a devastating fire the new location is even better than before. Check it out!!

~~

Cryptic Comments

**She's always late,
her ancestors arrived on the Juneflower.**

Specialty Drink

Broken Down Golf Cart Shooter

Ingredients: 1 shot Amaretto

1 shot Medori (melon liqueur)

1 shot of Rose's Lime Juice

Method: Mix all ingredients in a cocktail shaker with ice.

Pour into shot glass.

Banana Killer

Ingredients: 1 shot Artic Banana Vodka

3 ounces virgin painkiller mix

(coconut cream, pineapple juice, orange juice)

Method: Mix and pour over ice.

Bat Cave Special

Ingredients: 1/2 shot Amaretto

2 shot Malibu coconut rum

2 ounce cranberry juice

1 ounce pineapple juice

Method: Mix all ingredients in a cocktail shaker with ice. Enjoy!

Marooned

George and Mable were from a small town in Ohio and had spent long winter months leafing through glossy sailing magazines dreaming of chartering a yacht in paradise. "If only we knew how to sail," moaned Mable.

A month later George was out on the water with a small sailing school in the Caribbean island of Tortuga, while Mable stayed ashore. George crammed in several years' worth of necessary sailing knowledge in just five days, "Well done, darling," she said, when George showed her his crisp new certificate. "Now we can rent a yacht and make whoopee. I've been doing a bit of research and I think "The Maroonings" is the best company to go with."

"Why do you like them the best?" asked Charlie.

"Well, they're about twice as expensive as anyone else so they must be the best," she said, "And I've seen them in all the magazines. "We don't want to take any chances on a substandard vessel."

Next day they managed to rent a half million dollar yacht for a week. "The lady at the desk took ages examining my credit card details and insurance documents and didn't even bother to look at my qualifications," said an astonished George. "I suppose they know an experienced sailor when they see one,"

On the morning of their departure a young man with tattoos and two rows of ear rings came aboard to 'show them the ropes.' "Hi, I'm Blewitt," he said, with breath reeking of rum. "Most people call me Blue."

"And where are you from?" asked Mable apprehensively.

"I'm a citizen of planet earth," said Blewitt with a broad Australian accent.

"And how did you end up here?"

"I haven't reached the end yet," said Blue with a smile. "Actually I was in the import/export business, boat sank, I floated in on a bale of …… …ummm … … … on a packet of cargo. The Maroonings were looking for experienced mariners so I got a job and here I am."

Blue started showing the intrepid couple around, "What time is Otto the pilot coming?" asked Mable. "We're almost ready to go."

"The auto pilot is here," said Blue pointing to a red button, without batting an eyelid. He was used to ridiculous questions.

"Oh dear," said Mable, "George was expecting a person."

George and Mable finally departed the dock managing only a small scrape on the topsides. Their cruise in paradise had begun.

They managed to sail to a pretty cove lined with palm trees and enjoyed several rum drinks and a barbecue at a local beach bar called 'Happy's.' The next day the engine wouldn't start and George called the charter company for help. After two days waiting George had got rid of his hangover but was starting a new one when he met Charlie.

Charlie, being a friendly fellow, offered to have a look at the problem and found that the fuel filter was full of water. He cleaned it out, bled the system and it started immediately. Then George and Charlie spent an hour at the bar celebrating the newly running engine. It was then that Charlie found out that George had reported to the charter company that they were in Peter Island's Little Harbor whereas in fact they were at the Bight on Norman Island.

"Seems like there are plenty of ways to get marooned in the islands," slurred George, who seemed to be thoroughly enjoying himself. He was becoming a seasoned 'bareboater.'

Kong Ming Asian Terrace

Kong Ming Asian Terrace

Located at the Harbour View Marina Complex
Quality Asian Menu • Relaxing Waterfront Setting
Overlooking the Harbour
Delightful Decor and Quiet Oriental Music
'Take Outs' available

Tel: 495-1174 • VHF CH: 16

Giveaway coupon in back!

Kong Ming Asian Terrace

Kong Ming was a hero in China
Now his name's on an upper-crust diner
Wherever you're from
You just might live on
With a legacy like this, nothing's finer

Transport yourself to the east
For pleasure beyond measure, 'tis the least
You can do
For your fun-loving crew
They're guaranteed to be very pleased

The Kong Ming has an elegant style
Nothing like it for many a mile
Have soup, a Prawn Mee
Or Iced Sake, Lychee
The Kong Ming's at the top of the pile

Cryptic Comments

Banging your head against a wall burns 150 calories per hour... so keep trying the bike machine!

Kong Ming Asian Terrace

Here is an Asian restaurant of quiet sophistication and elegance. The décor transports you to the Far East while soft Oriental music adds to the overall ambience of peace and tranquility. A team of chefs in crisp whites with tall hats are visible from the dining area busily stirring their woks and working their stir fries while pretty waitresses see to your every need. If you're fed up with the Caribbean's ubiquitous 'fish, chicken or ribs' selections here you can choose from such delights as Manchurian Lamb, Cantonese Roast Duck, or, for the vegetarians, Szechuan Bean Curd or Garlic Eggplant.

This delightful restaurant with large dining patio looks out over the bay with a panoramic view of the harbour and cooling trade wind breezes. The islands on the south side of the Sir Francis Drake Channel can be seen in the background.

The Harbour View marina and dinghy dock make this restaurant ideal for yachtsmen and their crews. Midway between Norman Island and the Trellis Bay, Marina Cay anchorages this stop at Fat Hog Bay is perfect. There are mooring balls in the harbour, a Riteway supermarket just down the road, an ATM machine and a breakfast eatery. And if you need to top off with water and diesel/gas that's available too.

For those wishing to eat aboard, order a delicious Chinese take-out – they stand by on Ch. 16. so order in advance and just dinghy in to pick up. You can have Sweet and Sour Pork, Szechuan Beef, Manchurian Fish or Hong Kong Shrimp…to name just a few choices. Portions are huge and the prices are right – nothing over $15.00 on their take-out menu and each dish comes with vegetables and fried rice.

Specialty Drink

<u>Ice cold Sake garnished with a lychee</u>

Warm Sake by the carafe is available to accompany your dinner.

~~

Tides

Tides, the vertical movement of the sea, according to the position of the sun and moon, present a constant enigma to many, especially to those who live in the middle of a large continent like America.

Four farmers from Kansas had rented a large, expensive power yacht for a week. They arrived at the boat, had a quick tour with basic instructions and soon they were seated in the main salon with a deck of cards and a bottle of Jack Daniels. The conversation picked up as the contents of the bottle decreased and in between rounds of poker the facilities and amenities on board were discussed. Then a well fed, round faced young gentleman piped up, "I like these here windas," he said looking at the port holes just behind the settee." When the tide comes in we'll be able to see the fish swimming by."

He was serious, too.

Cybercafé

Giveaway coupon in back!

"Fireball Full Moon Party"
Great Breakfasts • Sandwich Lunches
Fresh Fruit Smoothies
Open for dinner
"Broadband Wireless Hotspot"

Tel: 495-2447 • VHF: CH 16 • www.windsurfing.vi

Cybercafé

A crazy time can be had
And the girls tend to be bad
It's not too soon
Because it's full moon
And everyone's a little bit mad

It's lunar-tic time at Trellis
The party you can embellish
Dance to the band
With your toes in the sand
Laugh with the jumbies, be devilish

The food is West Indian style
The BVI's best, by a mile
If you don't like goat water
Try it here, 'cos you ought ta
You wont see it again for a while

Cryptic Comments

Despite the cost of living, have you noticed how popular it remains.

Cybercafé

The Cybercafe is one of the coolest bars and restaurants in the BVI. Located in Trellis Bay next to Aragorn's art studio it opened for business in October '01 and is now a BVI tradition. The small bar and eatery was the brainchild of Jeremy Wright, long time water sports enthusiast and windsurfing aficionado who saw a market for cyber communications and decided to incorporate it with a unique food and drinks café. Customers can sit outside in the shade overlooking the bay while enjoying unusual creations at breakfast, lunch or dinner.

There's a special island menu with bar drinks and fruit smoothies with local tropical fruits. Breakfasts can be a simple affair of muffins and coffee right through to "The Full Monty." Yep, you guessed it – a full English breakfast. Unusual items on the "24 hr meals" menu are "Croque Monsieur," an open sandwich with seven-grain bread, ham, egg and cheese and Caribbean desserts. There are daily specials too, Caribbean style.

The Trellis Bay full moon parties, jointly hosted by the Cybercafe and Aragorn's Studio, are now the most popular party events on the island. A buffet of local Caribbean dishes is offered at a reasonable price, live fungi music or the sounds of a steel band can be enjoyed while dancing in the sand and unique burning fireball sculptures light up the night sky. As a climax to an incredible evening watch the antics of acrobatic mocko jumbies entertain the crowd late into the evening. This is one happening event not to be missed.

One minute from the airport the café is described as "the world's best departure lounge."

Specialty Drink

The Fruit Smoothie

Ingredients: 2 shots amber rum

1 banana, 1 mango, soursop, pineapple or other tropical fruit

1 scoop vanilla ice cream (optional)

Method: Blend all ingredients with a cup of crushed ice.

Garnish with a maraschino cherry.

Cryptic Comments

Sow your wild oats on Saturday night... then on Sunday pray for crop failure.

B.E.Y.C.
Pub

The Bitter End

Sports Bar with Pool, Darts, Foosball and Bar Games!!
Draught Beer on Tap • 'Build Your Own Pizza'
'All Day Menu' • Four Big Screen TVs
Hours: 11.30 a.m. to 10 p.m.
Specialty Drinks are offered daily.

Tel: 494 3152 • "Quarter Deck Marina" vhf ch 16 • www.beyc.com

Giveaway coupon in back!

The Bitter End

For the world's Number One water sports
Look at Virgin Gorda's resorts
The Bitter End
Is the perfect blend
Of water sports of all sorts

They have sailing and kite boarding too
You can fly to the sky where it's blue
The problem might be
Landing back on the sea
It's happened to more than a few

The strings are on demand
They're there, at your command
Don't be a clown
Pull one and come down
Just make sure you're not over land

Wind surfing is always a treat
It's available here, it's so neat
Join in the Hi Ho
Then to islands you'll go
But to win this event is a feat

Cryptic Comments

Playboy Bunny:
"Sex is like snow: you never know how many inches you're going to get or how long it's going to last."

Pub

The Bitter End

The Bitter End has justifiably earned the reputation of being the best water-sports resort in the Caribbean. Now the Bitter End's pub is fast following that reputation as being the best watering hole or 'happening place' in the BVI. It is located just across from the resort's small marina and caters to yachtsmen and guests who prefer a more informal atmosphere than the resort's more elaborate restaurants. Tables and chairs are located in the garden under shady flamboyant trees and overlook the marina, which is often occupied by expensive, luxury yachts.

The Pub now offers a large menu of varied and delicious selections. At lunch you can have a flying fish sandwich or choose from a list of mouth watering burgers, hot dogs and salads. At dinner choose a steak or a hunk of fresh fish, blackened or 'how-you-like-it.' A popular choice for a meal anytime is pizza. The natural brick oven is always on the go and patrons are invited to 'build-your-own pizza.' In fact if you arrive at an odd time don't worry, besides pizza there's an all-day menu. Regular hours are 11.30 a.m. to 10 p.m.

Besides the friendly wrap around bar where pints of ice cold draught beer are a popular choice, there is a large recreation room with pool (not the swimming version, the other one), foosball, darts and board games. For those wishing to watch their favorite sporting event there are at least four large TVs. On Monday nights a local DJ pumps up the volume and there's dancing under the stars.

Specialty Drink

Specialty Drink: The Bitter End has a new program for people to send in their favorite drink recipe, preferably from their yacht club back home. Here's one that was sent in many years ago in honor of Buddy Melges, winning skipper of the 1992 America's Cup.

The Bitter End Buddy

Ingredients: 2 shots 156 proof rum

                    4 ounces pineapple

                    4 ounces guava juice

                    squeeze of lime

Method: Mix all ingredients in a shaker and pour over ice cubes.
Finish with grated nutmeg and garnish with a maraschino cherry.

Cryptic Comments

Sex is hereditary. If your parents never had it chances are you won't either.

The
Bath and Turtle
and martini bar at Chez Bamboo

Lunch Menu with Tapas.
Virgin Gorda's premier bar, restaurant
and night spot.
New Open-air bar overlooking the marina.
Next to the marina in the heart of Spanish Town.

Tel: 495-5239 • VHF: CH 16 • Tel: 495-5752 • Chez Bamboo

The Bath and Turtle

A wonderful creature, the turtle
They're slow but ever so fertile
They lay hundreds of eggs
But the turtle regs
Say 'fishin' we have to curtail'

They make tasty soup, even stew
Turtle burgers and meat balls too
They look so cute
So the reason is mute
"Save the turtle" while we still have a few

So turtles feel at home around here
They'll enjoy a rum punch or a beer
Belly up to the bar
Daddy Turtle's the star
"Here, have a beer, there's no fear."

Cryptic Comments

The first thing to know about a 'survival situation' is not to get into one.

The Bath and Turtle

The Bath and Turtle now has a new 'Rendez-vous' bar overlooking the marina. The new bar is situated in a garden setting and is perfect for watching the comings and goings in the marina. The bar is designed along the lines of a traditional British pub and there is an extensive patio area for dining, cleverly decorated with vines on trelliswork and with shrubs and plants separating nooks and crannies for privacy. On Wednesday evenings a local live band plays and dancers turn the venue into a lively "jump up," heating up as the evening progresses.

Breakfast, lunch and dinner are available. One of the best day trips in the BVI is organized by the pub: Round trip ferry service from Tortola to Virgin Gorda and transportation to The Baths. Lunch is provided and a free rum punch is thrown in…all for a most reasonable price.

~~

Cryptic Comments

Ambidextrous: Can use either hand.
Ambidickerous: Likes either sex.

Specialty Drink

Super Sensation

Ingredients: 1 shot Myers rum

        1 shot Malibu coconut rum

        1 shot Triple Sec

        2 ounces pineapple juice

        squeeze of fresh lime

        soda water

Method: Mix in a shaker with ice all the ingredients except the soda. Pour into a tall glass over ice cubes and top up with soda water. Garnish with a maraschino cherry, wedge of lime and a slice of orange.

Rum Boogie

Ingredients: 1 shot amber rum

        1 shot Triple Sec

        1 shot Amaretto

        squeeze of fresh lime

        Coca Cola

Method: Mix in a shaker with ice all the ingredients except the Coke. Pour into a tall glass over ice cubes and top up with Coke. Garnish with a maraschino cherry, wedge of lime and a slice of orange.

The End

The people that come to the Caribbean to enjoy yachting holidays are generally in the higher income levels. Typical are those in the medical profession, lawyers, computer techies and money managers. Most expect to be regaled by stirring sea stories or entertained by tales of local color and humor and as a yacht charter captain Charlie would do his best. And sometimes his efforts were reciprocated.

One day Charlie had a group of four single gentlemen on a sail training course; one was a doctor. Charlie had great trouble remembering the meanings describing the specialist professions of medical doctors. For years he thought a pediatrician was a foot doctor. A few days into the trip Charlie and his guests were having drinks in the cockpit and when the doctor explained that his specialty was endoscopy Charlie facetiously remarked that scoping out rear ends might be less desirable than sailing. Expecting a laugh and a joke at his expense he was surprised to learn that endoscopy is exactly that: procedures involving the gastrointestinal tract.

The subject soon sank to a rather low level, as it seems to do when Charlie's at the helm. In the end (no pun intended) he found out that there are many strange objects extracted from people's nether regions, although how they got there Charlie was discreet enough not to ask. The good doctor told him that he had personally relieved people of: a glove, a shoe! (from a patient in a mental ward, he admitted), false teeth on a regular basis, condoms and a padlock (those darned chastity belts are tough sometimes!).

In recent years tattooing has become very much in vogue. Popular places for such body adornments are often in areas 'where the sun don't shine.' It also seems that these tattoos are placed strategically for the amusement of those partners who engage in doggy-style sex. Doctor Bottom, as he became lovingly referred to by the rest of the crew, described a sampling of exhibits he'd been privileged to see while on duty.

"'U.S. Grade A. Prime,' was one," he explained, "but it wasn't! Another was 'Happy Christmas' tattooed on one buttock. I came sooo close to adding 'Happy New Year' to the other buttock," he said with a laugh. "My favorite was a tattoo of a miniature Pinocchio with the words printed underneath 'lie to me, lie to me.'"

Now, Charlie's not likely to forget the meaning of 'endoscopy.'

~~

Cryptic Comments

**The lottery is a tax on idiots…
or people who can't do maths.**

**We all have to keep fit we are told.
My old Mum started walking five miles a day
when she was 60.
Now she's 92 and we've no idea where she is.**

Medicine at Sea

Ever heard of a medication called 'Lipitor?' It's apparently a cholesterol reducing drug that'll clean out your pipes better than a Roto-Rooter. Side effects, though, are enough to put off the most arterially challenged person on the planet. The wonderful benefits of the drug may be overshadowed by: muscle problems, liver ailments, tenderness, weakness, fever, flu-like symptoms, abdominal pain, fatigue, yellowing skin or eyes, dark urine, pale stools... Yippee! I'll take a couple of gross. Seriously, though, would any right-minded person risk taking this stuff? Personally a couple of shots of 151 proof rum have always worked for me. Side effects – your jokes get a bit more raunchy.

Charlie was out sailing with some novices the other day. They were on an offshore passage-making course form Tortola to St Martin. The weather started out fine with light winds but as the evening turned into night the winds increased and the seas picked up. By midnight crew-member Joe was feeling sick. In the dark cabin he rummaged through his baggage to find a Scopolamine patch and stuck it on. Ten minutes later he up-chucked the contents of his stomach, "There goes my Lipitor," he mumbled.

"What's that?" asked Charlie. Joe explained, and later, when Charlie found out the possible, gruesome side-effects of the wonder drug, he wasn't surprised.

In the morning Joe was bemoaning the Scopolamine patch he'd used when someone noticed he'd actually put it on upside down. This led to some early morning hilarity rare on a boat pounding to windward in 6-foot seas.

"Hey what a great cure for diarrhea," said someone. "Just stick a patch on your bum."

"Better not put it on upside down."

"Yeah, and verbal diarrhea like you have, stick a patch on your tongue."

Ron, the third crew, was almost seventy years old. Apparently he had an enlarged prostate and was in and out of the head all night long, "I'm going to try a patch on my pecker," he said.

A couple of days later he was sure it was working.

And that just goes to show you that psychology may be the best cure in your first aid kit.

~~

Cryptic Comments

A concrete truck collided with a prison van on Route I 95.
Cops are looking for 12 hardened criminals.

Have you ever noticed?
Anyone going faster than you is an idiot.
Anyone going slower is a moron.

Fat Virgin Café

**Bistro Dining on the waterfront at Biras Creek
Island dishes • Rotis • Sandwiches • Salads
Fresh Fish • Burgers and more
Friendly service and great prices!**

Tel: 495-5923 • VHF: CH 16 • www.fatvirgin.com

Giveaway coupon in back!

Esther's Fat Virgin Café

"Big Drinks, Great Food, No Shoes"

A virgin gets ever so fat
When she eats like the restaurant cat
So put in your order
Become Virgin Gorda
The café is right where it's at

Here you can come as a geek
Or a long hair rock and roll freak
The price is right
At this café at night
Sail in to the bar at "The Creek"

Pirates might be here as well
Americans call it "just swell"
When the Sunsail fleet
Arrives here to eat
It could be a journey to hell

Cryptic Comments

I'm not into working out.
My philosophy: No pain, no pain!

Fat Virgin Café

The Fat Virgin Café in Virgin Gorda's North Sound opened its doors in 1999 and became an immediate success. The reason: Delicious bistro type meals at reasonable prices – a hard commodity to find in an area of expensive resorts and restaurants. The service is exceptionally friendly and efficient and the location, right on the water's edge on the west side of Biras Creek, makes your al fresco lunch or dinner a most pleasant experience. Their motto sums it up perfectly, "Big Drinks, Great Food, No Shoes."

~~

Cryptic Comments

In order to get a loan from the bank; you must first prove that you don't need it.

If everything seems to be coming your way you're probably heading the wrong way down a one way street.

Specialty Drink

Banger's Punch

Ingredients: 1/2 cup spiced coffee

1 shot unrefined strong white rum (Arundel's is a good one)

1/2 shot Baileys

1/2 shot Tia Maria

2 ounces full milk (optional)

Method: Mix all ingredients thoroughly in a blender until creamy. Pour over crushed ice or ice cubes. Garnish with a maraschino cherry.

Note: If spiced coffee is hard to come by use regular coffee and add freshly grated nutmeg and a small cinnamon stick.

Cryptic Comments

He who stays calm in the face of chaos doesn't understand the severity of the situation.

Castaways

Tortola's Newest Party Bar and Hotspot
Fun Sports Bar, Five TVs, Gourmet Burgers
Food till Midnight
Open Air Gazebo with Lookout
Souvenir Cups, T Shirts etc.

Tel: 494 8295

Giveaway coupon in back!

Castaways

Instead of enjoying a lift
You find you've been cast adrift
A mutinous crew
Put you in a stew
'tween captain and crew was a rift

You fetch up at a dock in a town
With a bar, the newest around
'The Castaways'
What a place to play!
And to think! You could have been drowned

At the top they have a great lookout
With a telescope I looked all about
Then a ship I spied
"Those rogues," I cried
"Hang 'em all," there can be no doubt

Cryptic Comments

Never stand between a fire hydrant and a dog.

Castaways

Castaways is Tortola's newest hot spot and is located right in the centre of Road Town opposite the ferry dock. The bar is made from an old wooden sailboat, the topsides of varnished wooden planking and the counter a thick transparent epoxy covering pirate memorabilia and rib ticklin' jokes. The nautical theme carries on throughout the restaurant/bar and an open air 'lookout' or 'crows nest' provides a great view of the harbour. The original mast has been replaced with a stainless steel pole where volunteers

(hopefully pretty girls) are invited to strut their stuff at a 'pole dance' for prizes and drinks.

This is a 'fun' party bar.

The bar also displays popular sporting events. With five TVs and two satellite dishes, there's a choice of over 300 stations.

Castaways has a unique menu of gourmet burgers, half pounders every one! From beef, lamb, turkey, veggie etc. and all are served with fries and salad. Ever tried a juicy beef half-pounder with melted Brie dribbling down the sides – or a lobster burger with a piquant mayonnaise?

Food is served till midnight seven days a week and this party hot spot is open till 3 a.m. on Fridays. Then there's a whole range of specialty drinks that are served in souvenir cups. Downstairs the T shirt boutique has your take-home souvenirs and presents.

Specialty Drink

Surf's Up

Ingredients: 1 Shot Malibu Coconut Rum
1 Shot Blue Curacaou
Pineapple Juice
Cranberry Juice.

Method: Mix all ingredients in a cocktail shaker over ice. Pour over ice cubes and ENJOY!

'Jumbies' Bar at Leverick Bay

New Docks, Refurbished Marina
Sumptuous Menu, Fresh Fish Daily, Succulent Desserts
"NEW" Jumbies Beach Bar
Friday Night Beach Party: BBQ, Band, Mocko Jumbies
Prime Rib and Live Music on Saturday

Tel: 495-7154 • VHF: CH 16

Giveaway coupon in back!

'Jumbies' Bar at Leverick Bay

Leverick Bay on some days
Plays host to the mocko jumbies
With very long legs
Like wooden pegs
Some say they're African zombies

They put on a hell of a show
After the buffet, you know
There's roasted meats
And West Indian treats
Enough for a tropical glow

The show is right on the sand
Reggae is played by the band
After some rum
You want to have fun
But she'd rather relax and be fanned

Cryptic Comments

A Smith and Wesson beats four aces.

'Jumbies' Bar at Leverick Bay

Situated at Leverick Bay and nestled into a small natural cove the restaurant/bar is the centerpiece of a beautifully designed mini village of shops and service oriented businesses. There is a comprehensive water sports facility complete with parasailing. There is a scuba center, coffee shop, cyber café as well as a Laundromat, Spa, grocery shop and quality gift shops. From here there is road access to the rest of Virgin Gorda.

A 'new' beach bar, "Jumbies" is delighting visitors and locals alike. Situated on the sand with attractive gazebos and adjacent to the swimming pool this new attraction features special evening events with the highlight being the sumptuous buffet on Friday nights. A band provides dancing music after dinner and mocko jumbies entertain with acrobatic antics.

Owner Alex Yates is hell bent on providing an extremely high standard of food and service. Alex is a college trained professional chef and serves a large variety of fresh seafood dishes daily. On Saturdays hefty portions of prime rib are on the menu and live music entertains you into the wee hours.

There is also a mini market, which is called "The Chef's Pantry." The food store will concentrate on a good selection of deli goods and quality meats and fish so that boats and villas can provision from a professional chef's kitchen.

The Restaurant at Leverick Bay is a delightful dinnertime eatery with central bar and tables on the veranda overlooking the sound. Downstairs a poolside bar and restaurant serves pizza, sandwiches and burgers at lunchtime and your favorite tropical drink can be enjoyed while swinging from the unique hanging lounges by the freshwater pool.

Specialty Drink

The Leverick Bushwacker:

Amber rum

Kahlua

Amaretto

Bailey's Irish Cream

Mix together equal parts of the ingredients. Serve over ice. Add a scoop of vanilla ice cream for that extra creamy taste.

Cryptic Comments

The repairman will never have seen a model quite like yours before.

Wendell's World

Eat, Drink, Relax. Listen to Wendell himself on guitar
Beach Bar • Boutique
Jost Van Dyke
... it's all about limin' on Jost Van Dyke !

PH: 495-9969 • VHF: CH 16

Wendell's World

Wendell plays the guitar
Calypso can be heard from afar
His bar's the new fad
He sounds like his dad
That's Foxy, of the Tamarind Bar

Great Harbour is the name of the place
On Jost Van Dyke's south face
At the end of the day
It's the place to play
Or relax at a much slower pace

Cryptic Comments

The face is familiar
but I can't quite remember my name.

Wendell's World

Wendell's World is right on the beach in Great Harbor, Jost van Dyke next to Foxy's. It's an island bar in the truest sense of the word with a palm frond covered back porch on the sand and wooden benches and tables to sit at while enjoying a simple lunch or a frosty beer. Just opposite is the gift shop with unusual souvenirs, jewelry from the Amazon and Africa and artwork from other Caribbean islands.

The restaurant specializes in barbecue and fresh fish.

Wendell has now slipped into his father's shoes and sometimes entertains the crowd with song and guitar.

~

Cryptic Comments

Tell a man there are 20 million stars and he'll believe you.
Tell a man there's wet paint on that bench he's about to sit on and he won't believe you.

Specialty Drink

Pink Windy:

Ingredients:

> 1 shot each of the following:
> Coconut rum
> Banana rum
> Mango rum
> Orange rum
> White rum
> Fruit Punch
> Lime
> Nutmeg

Method: Mix all the ingredients (except lime and nutmeg) in a cocktail shaker with ice. Pour over ice and serve with a wedge of lime and freshly grated nutmeg.

Cryptic Comments

The more people I meet the more I like my dog.

Neptune's Treasure

"Freshest fish in the BVI because we catch it!"
Huge lobster dinners!
Family run guest house with A/C rooms

Tel: 495-9439 • VHF: CH 16
www.neptunestreasure.com

Giveaway coupon in back!

Neptune's Treasure

It's called the 'Dark and Stormy'
It'll make you hot and horny
Not the Race
But the name of the place
Says the waitress, and she's from 'ere

It's made from Gosling's rum
The best rum under the sun
Add ginger beer
It becomes clear
You'll have dark and stormy fun

Sal's a dark skin beauty
A Caribbean cutie
A drink or two
Then right on cue
You'll see her shake that bootie

Cryptic Comments

Dancing is a vertical expression of a horizontal desire.

Neptune's Treasure

Neptune's Treasure is a family success story unmatched in the BVI. Vernon and Julie Soares, of Portuguese descent, came to the BVI from Bermuda in the late 60s and began a fishing business in Jost van Dyke. It wasn't long before they realized that the best fishing was in Anegada and Neptune's Treasure was born. The primary fishing was longlining for swordfish and soon the family were supplying the whole of the BVI. In 1973 a small bar was established on the property at Setting Point and a restaurant soon followed – serving mostly seafood, of course. Now there's a guesthouse, an expanded bar and restaurant with deck, a bakery, a campground, and a successful fishing business continues.

Every year Neptune's Treasure hosts the Dark and Stormy race weekend which takes place in March as a fun weekend with informal racing from Tortola to Anegada and back and a rest and relaxation day in between with all kinds of beach games and side trips.

~

Cryptic Comments

If love is blind why is lingerie so popular.

Specialty Drink

Dark and Stormy

Ingredients: 1 shot Goslings rum in an 8-ounce glass

top up with Barritts ginger beer

Note: This is a Bermuda classic

Anegada Sunset

Ingredients: 1 shot peach schnapps

1 shot Grand Marnier

1/2 ounce grenadine

2 ounces orange juice

Method: Mix well together and pour over ice cubes.

Garnish with a maraschino cherry.

Cryptic Comments

Time is wasted when you're wasted all the time.

The Big Bamboo

"Voted Best Bar and Restaurant" 2003 Trophy
Anegada's *First* North Side Beach Bar!
Spectacular Beach • Good Snorkeling • Great Beach Bar
Island Style Lunches –
lobster, fresh fish, conch and more!

Giveaway coupon in back!

Tel: 495-2019 • VHF: CH 16 • Cell: 499-1680 (beach)

The Big Bamboo

The bar is right on the beach
But not within easy reach
Without much fuss
Take an open air bus
And a drink for the crew, one each

The turquoise sea is a sight
The sand, a sparkling white
The Big Bamboo
Will look after you
For years they've been doing it right

It's the greatest place to have lunch
That's a fact, not just a hunch
Lobster is here
So is cold beer
Or have their special rum punch

Cryptic Comments

An invisible man married an invisible woman: the kids were nothing to look at either.

The Big Bamboo

On the north side of Anegada on one of the BVI's most beautiful beaches, Loblolly Bay, you will find The Big Bamboo. The bar and lunchtime restaurant has a steady stream of customers mostly from the yachtsmen that visit Anegada and then transit the island by mini bus to enjoy the sweeping sandy beaches and fantastic snorkeling of Anegada's north shore. There are hammocks slung from seagrape trees and shade umbrellas just above the high watermark. There is always a good supply of delicious fresh seafood at the restaurant; conch, fish and lobster. The bar has some of the most imaginative drink specials on the island. One is the Anegada Davida, named for the famous rock song of the 70s, and apparently is a shortened form of "In de garden of Eden." Say it quickly and you'll see what I mean.

Another song associated with the Big Bamboo is probably the most famous calypso ever written. Here are some sample verses:

The Big Bamboo

I asked my lady what should I do,
To make her happy not make her blue
She said, "The only thing I want from you,
Is a little bit of de big bamboo."

I sold my lady a banana plant
She said, "I like it, he elegant
We shouldn't let he go to waste
But he's much too soft to suit my taste."

She met a China man, Him Hung Low
They got married, went to Mexico
But she divorced him very quick
She said, "I want bamboo, not chopstick."

Specialty Drink

Anegada Davida

Ingredients: Another secret recipe. This one contains an assortment of exotic liqueurs mixed with lychees or Chinese gooseberries. Blended with crushed ice you'll probably want a second round of these.

Big Banana Teaser

Ingredients: A mix of Myers dark rum, Kahlua, orange, pineapple, guava and grapefruit juices – shaken and poured over ice. Again the proportions are secret.

Cryptic Comments

If a man does not keep pace with his companions, perhaps he hears a different drummer.

Names

What's in a name you might well ask? Well, for sailors who have just launched their new yacht (or newly acquired yacht) the christening of it is of primary importance. It is how you and your yacht will be perceived.

There are definite categories that boat names slot into. There are the funny ones, the romantic ones, the sexy ones, the erudite ones, the ones that signal a financial windfall and those that honor a wife or daughter.

Of all the names out there most use the 'double entendre.' Wet 'n Wild is one of my all time favorite boat names and conjures up exciting sailing and kinda challenges female crew members. The racing boat 'Slippery when Wet' comes into the same category as does 'Foreplay.' Some boaters can be cunning linguists... "Go to slip 69, starboard side to"

'Sailbad the Sinner' must be a re-incarnated pirate. 'Passing Wind' elicits a laugh at first glance but after that you are tempted to anchor upwind of him. 'Never Again' is rather clever because it reminds all of us that we have at one time or another sworn to 'never do this again.' But then the memories of magic moments tend to overshadow the nightmares and we find ourselves once again back at the helm. There's even a 'Never Again 2.'

The yacht name 'Pair o' docs' denotes that the owners are a pair of medical practitioners and perhaps the paradox might be that two docs could never be on a sailing vacation at the same time.

Some yachties favor names of Greek gods, planets or constellations. A friend of mine named his boat Aeolus, the Greek god of the wind. When he started chartering everyone wanted to know the history and story of Aeolus. The poor captain became so bored with the re-telling of the same story over and over and over that eventually he told his inquisitive guests, "Aeolus means anal sex." That put an end to any further enquiries.

Those who have had cash windfalls sometimes pass on the message. 'Wall Street,' 'Arbitrage,' even '.com' have been seen in anchorages recently but somehow the aura of cold capitalism fails to inspire any warmth or camaraderie of the sea. Some one less fortunate named his boat 'Aloan at Last.' One can envision a guy who has lost the house, the car and the life savings but never-the-less has cut the unwanted ties.

In a similar vein some choose acronyms. 'Fujimoh' is not a Japanese General but rather F#$% you Jack I'm outa here.

If you're not careful you might send out the wrong perception entirely. Charlie named his first boat 'Prudence' and everyone thought he was being a bit prudish. Really, though, he had named it after a particularly ravishing young beauty from Belize who 'danced like a flower in the wind.' Perhaps he should have named her Windflower instead.

And lastly there are those who attach no significance whatever to a boat's name but they are really the exceptions. Anyway, who cares? And, believe it or not, 'Who Cares' is the name of a large power yacht seen recently in the BVI.

For me a clever, witty or romantic name is a pleasure... like 'Dancing Bare,' which has nothing to do with Winnie the Pooh.

~

Cryptic Comment

Great scientists say the universe is never ending, so how can it be expanding?

The Cow Wreck

Cow Wreck Bar

Cow Wreck Bar

I'd rather go swimmin'
With bow legged women
Then swim right through their knees
The bearded clam
I grab if I can
I always try my best to please

I'd rather go fishin'
Stay at Li'l Bit Inn
Then eat on the deck
Of the bar called Cow Wreck
Ride really fast
On a Little bit T'az
It's the name of the boat they go fishin' in

Cryptic Comments

On the other hand you have different fingers.

The Cow Wreck Cow Wreck Bar

First prize in all the islands goes to this bar for its original theme and name. Anegada, popularly known as a graveyard of ships, did lay claim to a ship whose cargo was a hold full of cow bones that were destined for a glue factory in Europe. The ship, the *Rocus*, sank near the southeastern end of Horseshoe Reef in 1929 and the iron ship still makes an interesting dive, although somewhat eerie with so many bones strewn around on the ocean floor. The Cow Wreck Bar and Grill is nowhere near the wreck site but is located on Anegada's north shore on a spectacularly beautiful beach and apparently near another shipwreck full of bones. Coincidentally there is an area of quicksand nearby that has caused the demise of several cattle. Also perfect for the Cow Wreck theme. Bones and skulls decorate the bar along with fishing floats, nets and other fishing paraphernalia.

This bar/restaurant is famous for its giant lobster feasts and wonderful views over the breaking reefs, especially on full moon nights. The Cow Wreck Resort now offers villas to rent, right next to the beach. Scooters are available too; a perfect way to explore the island.

Specialty Drink

Wreck Punch

Ingredients: Antiguan white rum

assorted fruit juices

Method: There seems to be a conspiracy afoot in Anegada because everyone wants to keep their drink recipe secret. Perhaps it's a marketing ploy to make you try one.

Cryptic Comments

Why should I do anything for posterity?
What has posterity ever done for me?

How to Shower:

Like a Woman

1. Take off clothing and place it in sectioned laundry hamper according to lights and darks.
2. Walk to bathroom wearing long dressing gown. If you see your husband along the way, cover up any exposed areas.
3. Look at your womanly physique in the mirror – make mental note – must do more sit-ups.
4. Get in the shower. Use face cloth, arm cloth, leg cloth, long loofah, wide loofah and pumice stone.
5. Wash your hair once with Cucumber and Sage shampoo with 43 added vitamins.
6. Wash your hair again to make sure it's clean.
7. Condition your hair with Grapefruit Mint conditioner enhanced with natural avocado oil. Leave on hair for fifteen minutes.
8. Wash your face with crushed apricot facial scrub for ten minutes until red.
9. Wash entire rest of body with Ginger Nut and Jaffa Cake body wash.

Like a Man

1. Take off clothes while sitting on the edge of the bed and leave them in a pile.
2. Walk naked to the bathroom. If you see your wife along the way, shake wiener at her making the "woo-woo" sound.
3. Look at your manly physique in the mirror and suck in your gut to see if you have pecs (no). Admire the size of your wiener in the mirror and scratch your ass.
4. Get in the shower.
5. Don't bother to look for a washcloth (you don't use one).
6. Wash your face.
7. Wash your armpits.
8. Blow your nose in your hands, then let the water just rinse it off.
9. Crack up at how loud your fart sounds in the shower.
10. Majority of time is spent washing your privates and surrounding area.
11. Wash your butt, leaving those coarse butt hairs on the soap bar.
12. Shampoo your hair (do not use conditioner).

Like a Woman *continued*

10. Rinse conditioner off hair (you must make sure that it has all come off).
11. Shave armpits and legs. Consider shaving bikini area but decide to get it waxed instead.
12. Scream loudly when your husband flushes the toilet and you lose the water pressure.
13. Turn off shower.
14. Squeegee off all wet surfaces in shower. Spray mold spots with Tilex.
15. Get out of shower. Dry with towel the size of a small country. Wrap hair in super absorbent second towel.
16. Check entire body for the remotest sign of a zit, tweeze hairs.
17. Return to bedroom wearing long dressing gown and towel on head.
18. If you see your husband along the way, cover up any exposed areas and then sashay to bedroom to spend an hour and a half getting dressed.

Like a Man *continued*

13. Make a shampoo Mohawk.
14. Peek out of shower curtain to look at yourself in the mirror again.
15. Pee (in the shower).
16. Rinse off and get out of the shower. Fail to notice water on the floor because you left the curtain hanging out of the tub the whole time.
17. Partially dry off.
18. Look at yourself in the mirror, flex muscles. Admire wiener size again.
19. Leave shower curtain open and wet bath mat on the floor.
20. Leave bathroom fan and light on.
21. Return to the bedroom with towel around your waist. If you pass your wife, pull off the towel, shake wiener at her, and make the "woo-woo" sound again.
22. Throw wet towel on the bed. Take 2 minutes to get dressed again.

Sky Bar and Restaurant

Sky Bar & Restaurant

New Mouth-Watering Menu.
Large Selection of Tropical Cocktails,
Appetisers and Tapas Daily,
Best View in the Islands. Open 10am until…

Tel: 494 3567 • VHF: CH 16

Giveaway coupon in back!

Sky Bar & Restaurant

To get a little bit high
Have a drink up in the sky
Your soul will be revvin'
When you're that close to heaven
Then you'll have to come down… with a sigh

The view is one of the best
You can see to the east and the west
But do not look down
You'll get giddy, you clown
Sit down with a drink, have a rest

You can party till late at the 'Sky'
If you're lucky, they'll have a fish fry
It's an island tradition
When they've been fishin'
Specially when fish fly right by

Sky
Bar & Restaurant

The Sky Bar and Restaurant has been revisited – from the name change to new delectable offerings. From 10 am to late in the evening tropical cocktails can be enjoyed along with a wide variety of hors d'oeuvres and tapas, (that unique brand of Spanish delicacy with a Mediterranean flair). The best time to visit the Sky Bar is just before sundown when the breathtaking colors of a beautiful sunset can be enjoyed to the fullest.

Besides a 360 degree view you can browse the gift shop while waiting for a sumptuous dinner or a spread of your choices from the tapa menu.

~

Cryptic Comment

**A smile is a curve
that can set a lot of things straight.**

Specialty Drink

Pink Sky

Ingredients: 2 shots amber rum

1 shot Amaretto

2 ounces Coco Lopez

2 ounces pineapple juice

squeeze lime juice

dash of Grenadine

Method: Blend all the ingredients with a cup of crushed ice. Garnish with a maraschino cherry

Mountaintop

Ingredients: 2 shots amber rum

1 shot Amaretto

1 ounce Grenadine

1 banana

2 ounces simple syrup, squeeze lime juice

Method: Blend all the ingredients with a cup of crushed ice. Garnish with a slice of orange, a section of pineapple and a maraschino cherry.

Myett's

"Special Welcome to Yachtsmen"
Brunch, Lunch and Dinner in our garden restaurant
Breakfast in season. Happy Hour.
E-mail services • Laundry Facilities • Gift Shop • ATM
AC Rooms and Showers • "NEW" Spa Services.
Super new gift shop. "We be Divin'" Outlet.
Tel: 495-9649 • VHF: CH 16 • www.myettent.com

Giveaway coupon in back!

Myett's

This bar is right on the sand
The restaurant is never called bland
The requests for a wedding
Seem never ending
The setting is ever so grand

You guessed, it's at Cane Garden Bay
A most beautiful place to stay
Their brand new rooms
Are perfect for grooms
With new wives, "Come on down… and play."

Cryptic Comments

Deja Moo:
The feeling I've heard all this bull before.

Myett's

Myetts, on the beach at Cane Garden Bay, is a cleverly designed complex that uses natural surroundings, man-made gardens and tropical foliage to provide a truly Caribbean setting. Kareem Rhymer opened in 1992 and with wife Valerie has been expanding and improving the popular beach bar/ restaurant ever since. The location is far enough away from the crowds at the other end of the beach to afford some privacy and there's always a shady spot under the palms for a happy hour drink.

Myett's is open for lunch and dinner and at weekends there's live music with the band performing on stage at the end of the restaurant, ideal for dinner dancing. The complex houses a well-stocked gift shop, a communications center with Internet access, showers for yachtsmen, and rooms are available. Now the services of a spa are available for that special rub down or massage. If you feel like organizing a scuba dive "We be Divin'" has opened up a full service facility on the premises.

Myett's is also the venue for special events like "The Summer Jam," a mini music festival with bands performing from around the region.

~~~

Cryptic Comment

GUYS: No shirt, no service.
GALS: No shirt, no charge.

Specialty Drink

Myett's Delight

Ingredients: 1 shot Myett's Rum

Fruit Punch

Splash of Anana

Measure of Coco Lopez

Method: Blend all ingredients with cup of crushed ice. Serve in a long glass and finish with grated nutmeg

Cryptic Comments

Love grows by giving.
The love we give away is the only love we keep.

Anegada Reef Hotel

Starlight dinners on the sand!
Reservations by 4:00pm
Rooms available, yachtmen's rates.
Huge lobsters direct from the pen!
Other delicious choices available.
"Rum smoothies"
Tel: 495-8002 • VHF: CH 16 • www.anegadareef.com

Giveaway coupon in back!

Anegada Reef Hotel

The island is ever so flat
In fact it's as flat as a mat
And the water, it's thin
Take care when sailin'
Unless you arrive on a cat

At the reef they offer temptation
An Anegada sensation
No, it's not a flamingo
Or a game of bingo
It's that creepy crawly crustacean

So lime a while at the bar
Chat to a local iguanaar
He's unique so I'm told
So he'll probably be bold
"On this island," he'll say, "I'm the star!"

Cryptic Comments

A wolf in sheep's clothing needs professional help.

Anegada Reef Hotel

Anegada Reef Hotel is Anegada's only hotel. Located at Setting Point it is the centre of activity for yachtsmen and the occasional visitor to this unique and sparsely populated island. You can sense the difference when you approach the island by boat: the bases of the fleecy cumulus are tinged with turquoise and trees seem to grow out of the water on the horizon. The tallest point on Anegada is 28-ft.

Visitors come here for two main reasons: to sample the island's abundant lobsters and to snorkel some of the best underwater scenery in the Virgin Islands, off the north shore beaches. But there is something else Anegada gives to the itinerant visitor: a feeling of carefree abandon of almost dreamlike quality and a humility that large expanses of simple beauty can evoke… until you come back to reality with a "milk of amnesia" and a huge plate of baked lobster dripping with melted butter.

The small hotel/ bar/ restaurant has been running for nearly 20 years. The open-air dining area is just behind the sandy beach in a delightful tropical setting and breakfast lunch and dinner are available. If no one's around just help yourself from the bar and start a tab. A regular shuttle bus will take you to the north side beaches.

Specialty Drink

Milk of Amnesia

Ingredients: 1 shot vodka

                   1 shot Kahlua

                   1 shot Amaretto

                   2 ounces milk

Method: Mix all ingredients in a cocktail shaker.

                   Pour over ice and finish with freshly grated nutmeg.

Cryptic Comments

Shake it off, stomp it down and rise to the next level.

Bananakeet Café

Best BVI Sunset View by a long way!
Sunset Happy Hour with hors d'oeuvres
Large pool next to the patio bar/restaurant
Reservations requested for dinner.

Tel: 495 4100 • www.heritageinnbvi.com

Bananakeet Café

Bananakeet is a café
A yellowbird too, so they say
Come and stay cool
Jump into their pool
It'll be a most pleasurable stay

They have a spectacular view
Yellow, red, purple and blue
This sunset you'll like
Over Jost van Dyke
Don't miss it, whatever you do

There are rooms here that you can rent
And their dinner is 'heaven sent'
Stay for a while
And drink in style
An 'irie' time's what she meant

Cryptic Comments

Peace will never come until people realize there can be harmony in diversity.

Bananakeet Café

The Bananakeet Café at the Heritage Inn is one of Tortola's best kept secrets. It is situated on a ridge on Tortola's north side, just up from Carrot Bay and only minutes from Cane Garden Bay.

The dining area is organized around the pool and overlooks an amazing panoramic view. The hors d'oeuvres menu at happy hour includes coconut shrimp, wraps, chips and dips and more.

The inn has nine comfortable rooms each with its own spectacular view, and at very reasonable prices. This is a "must stop" spot!

~~

Cryptic Comment

Take delight in people's differences.

Specialty Drink

The Bananakeet:

Ingredients: Fresh Banana
                1 ounce Bailey's Irish cream
                1 ounce vodka
                Coconut cream
                Aphrodisiacal nutmeg

Method: Mix all the ingredients in a blender with crushed ice (or pour over ice cubes) except the nutmeg, Finish with grated nutmeg on top.

Smooth Passion:

Ingredients: Passionate-fruit juice
                1 ounce coconut rum
                1 ounce triple sec
                1 ounce amber rum
                Coconut cream

Method: Mix all the ingredients in a blender with crushed ice or pour over ice cubes.

Cryptic Comments

I'm going to say this just once, "I have nothing to say."

Pomato Point
Pomato Point Bar & Restaurant

Delicious Lobster Dinners
Great sunsets
Three miles of sandy beach.
Ask about our Beach Cottages

Tel: 495-9466 • VHF: CH 16

Giveaway coupon in back!

Pomato Point
Bar and Restaurant

On a long white sand beach
And I really don't want to preach
The Pomato Point
Is the best lobster joint
They've created their own special niche

Pink Flamingoes do fly
To their bar my, oh my!
Soakin' up sun
Saturated with rum
It's the specialty drink you must try.

Cryptic Comments

If you wish to avoid work, find a job you love.

Pomato Point
Pomato Point Bar & Restaurant

Pomato Point restaurant was one of the first in Anegada to cater to yachtsmen. It is located just to the west of Pomato Point, which carries shoal water some 50 yds offshore. However there's an ideal anchorage in about 8-ft of sand just off the restaurant and a pristine three mile sandy beach. Approach at 70 degrees magnetic or with Jost van Dyke on your stern. Beware of swells in inclement weather which can make the anchorage rolly especially in the winter months. The same delightful menu can be had at The Lobster Trap at Setting Point where the anchorage is more settled.

Pomato Point specializes in barbecued lobster on the grill. Huge portions are served, usually two halves of a big lobster, wrapped in foil and cooked in their own juices. You will likely be served baked potato, large salad, dessert and coffee.

A small museum of shipwreck artifacts takes up a small room in one corner of the restaurant.

Specialty Drink

<u>Pink Flamingo</u>.

Ingredients: 2 ounces amber rum

Splash of Bailey's Irish cream

Splash of coconut cream

Splash of pineapple juice

Splash of strawberry syrup

Method: Mix in a blender with crushed ice or stir together and serve over ice.

Cryptic Comments

A politician is someone who will
lay down your life for his country.

One Love

One Love

Seddy's is down the beach
It's not too far to reach
Just dinghy in
To the One Love inn
"Bushwhacker please! One each!"

You'll probably see fish fryin'
Maybe, hear baby cryin'
Tis a family space
And a Rasta place
"Another round! I'm buyin.'"

'No shoes, No Shirt, No Problem'
Became the beach bar's anthem
But then…Oh no!
The same logo
Appeared on Kenny's album

Now, even the sea birds
Know he stole those words
But enjoy the tricks
And One Love lyrics
And Kenny – Join the nerds!

Cryptic Comments

If you can't take the heat, don't tickle the dragon.

One Love

The "One Love" beach bar is down at the quiet end of Jost van Dyke's famous White Bay beach, known for its white, powdery sand and crystal clear turquoise water. You can't miss it. It's a true drift wood bar with flotsam and jetsam, fishing floats, lobster pots, nets – decorating both inside and out. The owner of the bar is Foxy's son Seddy and he seems to have inherited his dad's ability to entertain. Seddy performs amazing magic tricks, which are especially enjoyed by the kids. If you want your kids to disappear, take 'em along!!

Seddy's now has a brand new kitchen and lunch is served daily. Succulent ribs, chicken and fresh fish are served daily. Local composer and guitar maestro 'Ruben' plays daily Thursday to Sunday, 12 noon until…

~~

Cryptic Comments

Never hit a man with glasses, hit him with a baseball bat.

Specialty Drink

Seddy's Bushwacker

Ingredients: 1 shot amber rum

1 shot vodka

Coconut cream

Bailey's Irish cream

Kahlua

Amaretto

Method: Mix all ingredients in a cocktail shaker or jug and pour over ice. Garnish with a maraschino cherry.

Cryptic Comments

I am in favor of the metric system, every inch of the way

D' Best Cup
Trellis Bay

D' Best Cup

The Best Cup of Coffee in the Islands
Italian Ice Cream and Fruit Yogurt Smoothies
Home of the original 'Planter's Punch.'
Cold Beers and Drinks, Cuban Cigars

Tel: 495 0259

Giveaway coupon in back!

D' Best Cup

There's a shop in Trellis Bay
Where Black Sam Bellamy did stay
Cast all asunder
Rape pillage… and plunder
A punch at the end of the day

It'll delight the whole of the crew
Black Sam was smart, he knew
That d' Best Cup
Is the place to sup
And 'punch' is the best brew

Coffee is available too
In the morning…what else do you do?
A good cup o' Java
Makes the day start fasta
All day you'll be feelin' brand new

Cryptic Comments

France has always been there when they needed us.

D' Best Cup

D' Best Cup is an unusual café right on the strip at Trellis Bay. Its specialty is exotic coffees and you can have anything from espresso through to the finest latte. You can buy fresh ground coffee beans by the pound and enjoy it later at that perfect anchorage or just sit and enjoy a freshly brewed cup of joe on the outdoor patio. Also they serve delicious hot sandwiches for lunch. Try their fruit smoothies.

D' Best Cup also serves delicious home-made Italian ice cream by the cup or cone, or buy a party pack to eat after dinner on the boat.

Owner, Phillip Fenty hails originally from Grenada, the home of the Caribbean's famous Planter's Punch. Phillip doesn't serve up any old rum and fruit juice and call it rum punch. He is very particular in the ingredients and quantities for the famous Grenada drink, right down to the freshly grated nutmeg on top.

~

Cryptic Comments

Never underestimate the power of stupid people in large groups, especially at election time.

Specialty Drink

Planter's Punch (the real rum punch)

Ingredients: 1 oz. amber rum
                    2 oz. white rum
                    Simple syrup
                    Lime juice
                    Angostura bitters
                    Grated nutmeg

Method: There is a time honored ditty that governs the perfect mixing of this famous Caribbean cocktail: "One of sour, two of sweet, three of strong and four of weak." In this case that translates to one part lime juice, freshly squeezed of course; two parts simple syrup (sugar and water); three parts rum in the above proportions, and four parts water. D' Best Cup recipe calls for a few drops of angostura bitters to be stirred in and the drink poured over ice instead of adding water. That gives it a little extra "punch." The drink is finished with a little grated nutmeg and garnished with a maraschino cherry.

Cryptic Comments

Before giving someone a piece of your mind, make sure you have enough to spare.

Whistling Pines

Dine on the sand under the pines
Conch and Lobster Specialties 'Surf and Turf'
Pool Table
Ask about our Guest Cottages
Reservations by 4 p.m.
Tel: (284) 495 9521 • VHF: CH16 • Cell: 443 5864 / 544 3728

Giveaway coupon in back!

Whistling Pines

There's a very amenable host
And that is no idle boast
At 'Bilto's by Sea'
Rub your hands with glee
For the best seafood on the coast

You can dine right on the sand
Under the pines as you planned
Have a surf and turf
Or a turf and surf
It's their special and it's quite grand

Pull up to the rickety dock
Tis where all the boaters do flock
Have a special "Pine Punch'
With a fishy dish lunch
'Anegada!' Yeah, you does rock

Cryptic Comments

The only person to get everything done by Friday was Robinson Crusoe.

Whistling Pines
Whistling Pines

This beach front restaurant at Setting Point Anchorage lives up to its name; it's situated at the water's edge under the famous Anegada pines. It has its own dinghy dock and the outside bar is housed in a quaint little gazebo

Anegada is famous for two things: gorgeous stretches of sandy beach and the sweetest conch and lobster on the planet. Just look at the Whistling Pines' menu and you'll see how they offer the island's delectable delicacies. Mixed in amongst such mundane offerings as honey stung chicken and beef burgers are delicacies like Conch fritters, Lobster burger, Lobster fritter, Stew Conch and Cracked Conch.

On the dinner menu grilled Anegada Lobster is at the top of the list along with several fish dishes and a Seafood Alfredo. The 'Piece de Resistance' is the Surf and Turf: a healthy slice of New York strip with a half a lobster tail.

Owner/manager 'Bilto' is a most congenial host and will make certain you have a good time. The bar/restaurant is open every day and happy hour is from 5.30 to 6.30 pm.

A pool table is available for those who wish to play with their balls.

Specialty Drink

Pines' Punch

Ingredients: 1 shot Cruzan Gold

1 shot Myer's Rum

Equal amounts of Guava Juice

Pineapple Juice, Puerto Rican Punch.

Method: Pour over ice cubes, stir well. Garnish with grated nutmeg

Cryptic Comments

Be willing to give up what you are for what you can become.

Corsairs

Corsairs

Corsairs is a buccaneer bar
With a restaurant above par
Have fine 'belly timber'
You're sure to remember
Pirates are heard to say AAAaaarrrhh !

It's on the beach at Great Harbor
Don't even walk any farther
A tattooed biker
Is now a van Dyker
The portions couldn't be any larger

Here, the beer is served cold
Have one, go on in, be bold
There are pirates galore
They all come ashore
To Corsairs, it never grows old

Cryptic Comments

The trouble with political jokes is
how often they get re-elected.

Corsairs

Your hosts Vinny and Debbie welcome you to Great Harbor's newest restaurant and bar. Corsairs is almost smack bang in the middle of Great Harbour and just a minute's walk from the main jetty. It is one of the newest bar/restaurants in Jost van Dyke and it's already one of the most popular. The food is excellent at Corsairs. Professional chef "Smokin' Joe Kozik" prepares Italian and Tex Mex nightly specials as well as continental and Caribbean fare. Corsairs is proud to say that "Sobriety is not our priority." They put the naughty into nautical so belly up to the bar and have fun!!

~

Cryptic Comments

We are the people our parents warned us about.

Specialty Drink

Wench Juice

Ingredients: Wench Juice

Method: Acquire a ripe wench and use your imagination.

Cryptic Comments

A babysitter is a teenager acting like an adult while the adults are out behaving like teenagers.

Potter's by the Sea

Potter's by the Sea

'Barbecued Lobster' (Potter's specialty)
'Seafood Platter' (recommended)
Cool Atmosphere, Warm Ambience
On the Water
Live Music Some Nights

Tel: 495-9182 • VHF: CH 16 • Cell: 284-443-8776

Giveaway coupon in back!

Potter's by the Sea

Potter's by the Sea
Is the place for you and me
Their fresh fish
Is quite delish
Bring your company

Their dinghy dock is long
But probably not so strong
Don't fall in
You'll take a swim
"I'm wet" will be your song

Eating done, the band'll foller
The singer's good, he sure can holler
Reggae's the name
Of his singing game
You can hear them in Tortoller

Cryptic Comments

Talk is cheap because supply exceeds demand.

Potter's by the Sea

Right at the end of the government dinghy dock at Setting Point, Potter's couldn't be more convenient. At the water's edge you can literally wiggle your toes in the sandy shallows while sipping your before-dinner drink. This restaurant's theme is rustic indeed and patrons have taken to adding comments, jokes, rhymes and eulogies of the restaurant and Anegada on the walls and supports of the building. Potter himself is a very congenial host and welcomes guests with aplomb. As is normally the case in Anegada, customers to the islands' restaurants have to order in advance so that the lobsters can be taken from the pen, read their last rights and then prepared for the grill. This process takes time but it helps to speed up the service at dinner…and 'speed' is not a word commonly understood in the islands.

Menu choices at Potter's are slightly different. One favorite is the 'Seafood Platter,' a choice which includes shrimp, fish and lobster served with a garlic butter sauce. There is usually plenty of cold Pinot Grigio available. Grilled lobster is always the favorite choice but fish, steak, chicken and ribs are usually on the menu.

Specialty Drink

<u>Bushwhacker</u>　　　Recipe and Method: Don't ask! Just try one!

~~

The Lawyer

A divorce lawyer told the story of a married couple who ran up a bill of 100K and then at the last minute changed their minds and decided not to divorce. Apparently they were always terribly in love when they were out partying. They would go out at weekends, have a fine dinner, dance the night away in some club and after imbibing heavily would rush home and leap into bed with a bottle of vodka and have terrific sex until the cock (croaked) crowed. The rest of the week they hated each other. The stay of divorce lasted for a month and then they started proceedings all over again…for another large fee. It reminded me of the maxim: "My wife hates me when I'm drunk. I hate her when I'm sober."

Foxy's Taboo

"It's Good to be Bad"
"Mediterranean fare with flair"
Mooring Balls available • Dinghy Dock
AND, Foxy's famous draft "Born 'ere Beer"

Reservations requested: Tel:495 0218 • VHF: CH 16
www.foxysbar.com

Giveaway coupon in back!

Foxy's Taboo

If you want to relax and be cool
Take a walk to the Bubbly Pool
That natural Jacuzzi
Is great if you're woozy
In fact it's a JVD rule

A cow might say a loud moo
Then it might just go to the loo
Whatever you do
It's considered taboo
To step in a pile of cow poo

When you get there jump right on in
With no clothes, it's considered no sin
The bubbles will thrill ya
No one will bill ya
Be naughty, there won't be no tellin'

Cryptic Comments

The two most important rules of life.
1. Don't tell everything you know.

Foxy's Taboo

Foxy's Taboo is the latest sensation in Jost van Dyke's plethora of watering holes and eateries. The Taboo specializes in Mediterranean "fare with flair."

The new restaurant and bar are just across from the ever popular Sandy Spit and just a stone's throw from Sandy Cay (a long throw). There are mooring balls to tie up to and a dinghy dock for your convenience. Don't forget that moorings are free for a daytime stop so a lunchtime visit becomes even more appealing.

Close by is the famous "bubbling pool," a sort of natural Jacuzzi where waves are forced through small holes and crevices in the rocks and a natural bubbling pool results. It's best when a moderate swell is running. A small black and white dog will act as your guide.

~

Cryptic Comments

How am I supposed to love my enemies when I can barely stand my friends.

Specialty Drink

Born 'ere Beer

Ingredients: Foxy's own homemade brew. Order a frothy glass of cold light, amber or dark beer.

How to please a woman

Caress, praise, pamper, relish, savor, massage, make plans, fix, empathize, serenade, compliment, support, feed, tantalize, bathe, humor, placate, stimulate, stroke, console, purr, hug, coddle, excite, pacify, protect, phone, correspond, anticipate, nuzzle, smooch, toast, minister to, forgive, sacrifice for, ply, accessorize, leave, return, beseech, sublimate, entertain, charm, lug, drag, crawl, idolize, worship etc. etc.

How to please a man

Show up naked.

Emile's
Mexican Cantina

Mexican Specials
English Spoken
Margaritas 'How-you-like-'em'
'Take Out' available

Tel: 495-1775

Giveaway
coupon
in back!

Emile's Mexican Cantina

Come to a Mexican-tina
Have a taco or a burrito
This place at East End
Is the place to send
Your friends for a Mexican 'deenar'

The beer will be served ice cold
Then watch the evening unfold
Order tequila
It is the best healer
Don't miss it, cos now you've been told

Sit down and dine 'al fresco'
It's the style in all of Mexico
Hot chile pepper
Can make it taste better
In the morning you'll remember it's so

Cryptic Comments

Don't you think hard work must have killed *someone?*

Emile's Mexican Cantina

The BVI's only Mexican restaurant is located at East End opposite the Harbour View Marina. An informal atmosphere is the hall mark of this appropriately named 'Cantina' with dining on an open-air deck. Tasty Mexican meals are served by friendly staff at reasonable prices. Emile's has several choices of Tequila on offer and their Specialty Drink is the Margarita. Ice cold Mexican beer is also available.

One of the distinct advantages of eating 'Mexican' in the BVI is that Montezuma's Revenge is unheard of.

Menu items include Burritos, Fajitas, Enchiladas as well as perennial favourites like burgers and pizza. Fresh fish and other seafood are often on the menu. Call for Take Out.

This eatery is perfect for yachtsmen and boaters. Tie your dingy at the marina and the Cantina is just across the road.

~~

Cryptic Comments

I wish I could help the homeless but I don't know where they live.

Specialty Drink

Strawberry Margarita

Ingredients: 1 shot tequila

                 1 shot Triple Sec

                 Margarita mix

                 strawberry puree

                 floater of Grand Marnier

Method: Mix all ingredients together in a cocktail shaker with ice, reserving the Grand Marnier floater. Pour into glass and add floater or over ice cubes if desired.

Cryptic Comments

Travel at the speed of time: one second per second.

The
Tamarind Club

The Tamarind Club

The Tamarind Club
Is really the Hub
When it comes to Sunday Brunch
Dip in the pool
To keep yourself cool
Then return for their Monday lunch

They really care
It's a family affair
Try the Eggs Benedict
With a Bloody Caesar
Or a Bedroom Teaser
You'll soon be their newest addict

The ingredients in
Their 'drink of sin'
Will likely cause a bit of a stir
There's vodka and rum
Gosling's 151
No wonder it's called the 'Leg Opener'

Cryptic Comments

Tough times don't last, tough people do.

The Tamarind Club

The Tamarind Club, located at Josiah's Bay, is a small hotel and restaurant in a magical setting surrounded by tropical gardens and cool Caribbean breezes. There are nine charming rooms enveloping a beautiful pool with a swim-up bar.

The restaurant's menu changes daily and uses the freshest local and imported ingredients. It is open 7 days a week for breakfast, lunch, and dinner and specializes in brunch on Sundays. Enjoy Eggs Benedict, Ale-battered Fish and Chips, Salads, Eric's Famous BBQ Ribs, and much more. Dinner is a quiet candle-lit affair.

The Tamarind Club's bar, "The Center of the Universe," is a focal point in the lounge. Its beautiful stone work bar features unique lighting, charismatic music, and many unique drinks. Fun bartenders will serve until the last guests are ready to leave.

Reservations are suggested for Dinner and Sunday Brunch.

~~

Cryptic Comments

I don't try to achieve immortality by doing great works, I try to achieve it by not dying.

Specialty Drink

Leg Spreader (a unisex cocktail, *honest*)

Ingredients: (Amounts – depends on your mood......)

Light rum, Dark rum, Gold rum, 151 rum,

Vodka, Tequila, Peach Schnapps, Coconut rum,

Gin, Midori, Triple Sec, Grenadine, OJ, Pineapple,

Coco Lopez, Nutmeg.

Method: Mix how you like and as much as you like.

Serve over ice. Should have the desired effect.

Cryptic Comments

Solution to two of the world's major problems: feed the homeless to the hungry.

The Dove Restaurant

Giveaway coupon in back!

"NEW" Tapa and Sushi Bar
Open for Dinner – A la carte menu – Large wine list
Warm ambiance – enhanced by jazz
5 -7 pm. Every Day: Champagne Special: $3.00

Tel: 494 0313

The Dove Restaurant

The Dove in the middle of town
Is the best restaurant around
Famous for food
That's ever so good
It'll be the secret you found

Drinks are made with champagne
Have one and come back again
It'll give you pleasure
That you can't measure
You'll be so glad that you came

Blackbeard! He came with a thrust
He also came with a lust
He had it in mind
For a lady to find
One of the more 'upper-crust'

Blackbeard was a pirate most able
But his morals were somewhat unstable
When someone did shout
"Rum is all out!!"
He shot a round under the table

Cryptic Comments

**Crime does pay.
Ask a BV Islander with an eight dollar an hour
job and a half million dollar speedboat.**

RESTAURANT & WINE BAR

The Dove Restaurant

The Dove is a quietly sophisticated cottage restaurant in the heart of Road Town. The new restaurant has been converted from a traditional West Indian wood-framed house complete with hip roof and generates a warm and cozy ambiance. There is a small wrap-around bar and more seating on an outside deck under a mango tree – ideal for those who wish to partake of a glass or two of wine from their very extensive list, a large selection of which is available by the glass.

A brand new building now houses a 'Tapa and Sushi Restaurant' with the same excellent cocktails and wines together with first class service and attention to detail.

The a la carte menu features such things as Moussaka, Venison, Lamb Tagine, Char-grilled Ahi Tuna with Lime Wasabi and Jerk Salmon. Situated opposite the ferry dock it is ideally located for both dinner and lunch guests with ample parking close by.

~~

Cryptic Comments

Always try to be modest, and be proud of it!

Specialty Drink

__Ice cold French Champagne.__

~

Cryptic Comments

Jesus loves you,
but everyone else thinks you're an asshole.

My cousin is gay; he went to London
only to find out that Big Ben was a clock.

It's not an optical illusion. It just looks like one.

The Royal BVI Yacht Club

Casual Boater's Ambience
Al Fresco Dining on the Deck
Non members welcome for lunch, dinner and drinks.
Special: Overseas Membership Offered with World-Wide Reciprocal Rights.

Tel: 494 3286 or 494 8140 • www.rbviyc.net

The Royal BVI Yacht Club

If you feel like having a race
Sailing a course at a pace
Get in a boat
Then keep it afloat
And end up back at the base

The competition is sometimes insane
Go racing, come first, then again
The Queen named it 'Royal'
So be ever so loyal
Sign up! It's the name of the game

There are Optis and Lasers galore
And lots of fun, that's for sure
If you feel it does matter
Join in the regatta
Next week you'll be back for more

Cryptic Comments

A true friend stabs you in the front!

The Royal BVI Yacht Club

The Royal BVI Yacht Club has a wonderful and colorful history. The founding members were a fun, dedicated group of sailors looking for a way to consolidate their sailing and social ambitions. It all began in the spring of 1972, in a donated house when a group decided to have a yacht club and named it the British Virgin Islands' Yacht Club. By 1974, 100 members strong, the club was growing. Charlie and Ginny Cary, the founders of The Moorings, which was in its infancy then, offered the use of their recreation room at Fort Burt, and the Club moved there on 9 April 1974. Recognition and acceptance demonstrated themselves that year when the club became a member of the Royal Yachting Association and the West Indies Yachting Association.

The present and permanent clubhouse was completed in 1993. The land is leased to the RBVIYC by the BVI government for 25 years, with an option for an additional 25-year lease. It took only 20 years to finally find a permanent home, but this one's a beauty! The club's membership has increased and the racing is far more serious than before. The racing boats are more serious too, and that has given a boost to the club's events and regattas. By 1999, the official papers had been submitted and accepted to unite the BVI Yacht Club with Royal Clubs from around the world. As a Royal Club, the BVI is recognized and allows its members reciprocal privileges that would otherwise not be garnered.

The largest regatta for the club is the BVI Spring Regatta. Started 34 years ago, by the same founding members of the yacht club, the BVI Spring Regatta and Sailing Festival, held the first weekend of April, now hosts 140 boats with well over 2,500 people coming from all over the world to race in the Sir Frances Drake Channel. The Royal British Virgin Islands' Yacht Club has come of age.

The Club cordially invites visiting yachtsmen to come and enjoy the club. Have lunch, dinner or drinks and sign up to become an 'Overseas Member' for the extremely reasonable price of $155.00. (overseas family membership $300.00, two adults and two children). Then enjoy reciprocal rights (fun events, social nights, showers etc.) in literally hundreds of clubs around the world.

Specialty Drink

Rum Punch

Ingredients and Method: This Punch is the Royal version of the traditional West Indian Rum Punch. It has more exotic fruit flavors and is protected by a secret recipe. The RBVIYC is offering two of these for the price of one for anyone producing the book at the clubhouse bar.

Cryptic Comments

Never speak badly about yourself; your friends will always say enough on that subject.

Pirates' Bight

Lunch and dinner
Deck chairs on the beach
Gift Shop
After dinner party nightly.

Tel: 496 7827 • VHF: CH 16
www.normanisland.com

Giveaway coupon in back!

Pirates' Bight

There's treasure here to be found
It's probably close underground
Pirates, they ferried it
Then they buried it
We'll find it! Sssshhh, not a sound.

Now dig, right near the beach
The treasure should be easy to reach
I just can't wait
To find Pieces of Eight
I feel like ol' Edward Teach

Yeah, Blackbeard, that was his name
To Norman Island he came
Now a pirates' bar
Has a Happy Aaaarhh
And 'rum' is the name of the game

Cryptic Comments

Don't feel inferior.
100,000 sperm…and you were the fastest.

Pirates' Bight

At the head of the bay in Norman Island's Bight is the party bar and restaurant called Pirates' Bight. By day it's the favorite of the day excursion boats who often stop for lunch and drinks after snorkeling adventures or hiking over the island in search of buried treasure.

The Treasure Caves are a big attraction here: A chest of treasure was found in the southern most cave in 1910 and the finder became rich because of it. A bunch of English scallywags seized a shipload of treasure from a foundering Spanish galleon off a storm ravaged coast in North Carolina in 1750. A large part of it found its way to Norman Island where it was buried. The afore mentioned chest had been secreted away in the cave for 160 years!! A lot of treasure is still unaccounted for.

The famous Scottish author, Robert Louis Stevenson, found out about it and used many of the facts for his story "Treasure Island." You can read all about it in the fascinating book, "The Virgins' Treasure Isle" by, ahem, Julian Putley.

In the evening dinner specials include Baby Back Ribs, cooked just how you like them. There's shrimp curry with Creole or lemon and ginger sauce. Catch of the day is available as is fresh lobster with butter and lemon sauce. Favorites at lunchtime include West Indian Roti, Ben Gunn roast beef sandwich and lobster salad. Favorites at lunchtime include West Indian Roti, Lobster Salad and an array of burgers.

After dinner the party often goes on into the wee hours with dancing under the stars.

Specialty Drink

Bushwhacker

Ingredients: 1 shot vodka

               1 shot Amaretto

               1 shot Kahlua

               1 shot Irish Cream

               Dash Crème de Cacao

               Coco Lopez

Method: Mix all ingredients in a blender and serve over ice (Makes two drinks). This drink can be blended with crushed ice to make a delicious smoothie.

Cryptic Comments

You are weird...
but around here it's not noticeable.

The Mine Shaft Café

Open for lunch and dinner
Famous for BBQ ribs
Mini golf
Breathtaking Sunsets

Tel: 495 5260 • www.mineshaftbvi.com

Giveaway coupon in back!

The Mine Shaft Café

They came here looking for gold
Those Spaniards were ever so bold
But when they found copper
They knew 'twas a flopper
It's not worth much when it's sold

Whatever you do have a 'Cave In'
Tomorrow you'll say that she gave in
Drinking that rum
You're sure to have fun
Followed by some misbehavin'

Your drink will arrive from the ceiling
It gives you that real miners' feeling
On a rope down the shaft
I know it sounds daft
But those miners you now sure believe in

Cryptic Comments

A day without sunshine is like......night.

The Mine Shaft Café

The Mineshaft Café takes its theme from the nearby derelict copper mine. The mine originated in 1837 when 36 Cornish miners sank a shaft, eventually to a depth of 240-ft below sea level. Some 140 Virgin Island men were employed in mining the copper which finally became exhausted in 1862. The site, which includes extensive ruins, is in a beautiful location looking out over the Caribbean Sea to the south. It has been a National Park site since March, 2003.

This unique theme bar and restaurant, decorated in the style of an old copper mine, is renowned for its friendly atmosphere and casual ambiance. The sunsets from here are breathtaking. The location boasts both a sunset deck and an Atlantic deck and panoramic vistas can be seen through all points of the compass.

The menu is the same for lunch and dinner with their famous barbecue ribs being the specialty. Lobster pasta, steaks, seafood, wraps and taco salads are just some of the interesting items on the menu.

The mini golf course is a popular attraction and many visitors come for an afternoon game, happy hour drinks at sunset and then dinner. Hole in one gets a free drink!!

Specialty Drink

The Cave-In

The ingredients and method for making this drink are secret, except that there's a lot of rum in it. If you order one, a bucket containing the secret ingredients, is lowered from the ceiling by rope and pulley, in true mining tradition!

Cryptic Comments

Get a new car for your wife –
it'll be a great trade!

You Don't Get a Free Meal for Nothing

There's nothing like stopping off for a drop o' grog and a decent plate of belly timber after a day of trade wind sailing. Charlie often likes to stop off at his favorite local watering hole, Fatima's: the portions are huge and the service is …well…Island style. The menu is generously sprinkled with fried specialties like chicken, chips, Johnny cakes, fish, conch fritters. The cook, Colestorella, also makes goat water, bull foot soup, pigtail and other island delicacies.

One reason Charlie loves it is because the service is so slow that there's ample time to try every available drink in the place. When Colestorella finally waddles over with steaming plates of food the guests are either vociferously extolling the virtues and wonders of the BVI, telling each other filthy jokes, or slumped over, head on table, having a nap. One thing is for sure; no-one leaves Fatima's hungry. Once Charlie's guests were so satiated with food and drink they actually accidentally left the place without paying the bill. It was then that the speed picked up considerably; Fatima proved to everyone that the hundred yard dash was no stranger to her. She arrived at their parked car before they did, turned around and introduced them to a totally new vocabulary. Some of the words were 'tiefin, scunt, hunky and tink-you-is.' Charlie, in his usual diplomatic style, apologized profusely and told his charter guests to add an extra ten dollars to the total and finally all was well; the evening ended happily.

Charlie has always been well loved at Fatima's. He often brings in groups of six or eight charter guests and for this service he is rewarded with a free meal. Recently Fatima's has got into the habit of adding an inexplicable figure at the end of the bill. Then, under this is another figure, before the total is arrived at underlined at the bottom. Usually the well lubricated guests pay up without a second glance but once a guest challenged this fairly large figure of extras. This brought about considerable confusion with the waitress having to run back and forth to the kitchen several times, returning each time with a different explanation. First it was a tax but the guest knew there was no restaurant tax in the BVI. Then it was extra drinks but drinks were already charged for. Then it was service charge but that was already included at the end. Finally it was explained that it was actually a 'different' service charge. One was for the entire staff and the other was for the waitress. The exasperated guest then grabbed the menu and at the bottom it clearly said, 'Please tip your waitress generously. It is not included in the bill.' Then the waitress explained that the menu was an 'old' menu and the tipping system had changed. All eyes then turned to Charlie who was expected to solve the problem. Charlie shook his head and palms up explained in his most humble way and in great detail how expensive island living was. Finally nods of approval were given from around the table and the total was agreed upon. Charlie breathed a sigh of relief and thought, 'You don't get a free meal for nothing.'

Patience and Deaf People

You've probably often heard the oft quoted bit of conversation between two deaf people:

"Let's go for a walk,"
"Isn't it Windy?"
"No it's Thursday."
"Me too. Let's go for a drink."

I like old people, even deaf old people, but they sure can be funny sometimes. I'll never forget my old Mum who became quite deaf in her latter years. On one occasion the whole family was sitting down for Sunday lunch when she quietly rocked to one side and let go a fart. Being deaf she thought it was a silent one but we all heard it and when both my brother and I started laughing she looked me squarely in the eye and said, "Julian, if you have to pass wind please leave the room." She continued eating without batting an eyelid.

Charlie had two students on his last sailing course, one was deaf and the other was an Italian. Italians can be excitable at the best of times but if you mix deaf, sailing tuition and

Italian in the same pot you'll likely come out with a recipe for disaster. Charlie relayed the story like this:

"OK, bear off the wind,"

"What is bear off?"

"Turn to port."

"I no want go back to port"

"No, no, turn to the left."

"Yes, we have left. I no want go back to port."

By this time they were in irons. Charlie explained by gestures what happened and how to avoid the situation. Finally they managed to back the jib and all was well. An hour or so later it was time for reefing practice. It went like this:

Charlie: "Right, imagine a big storm is coming and we'll have to reef."

"We'll hit the reef?!! Where is reef?"

"No, no, we have to reduce sail"

Italian helmsman student to deaf partner: "Big storm coming. Put on life jacket."

Charlie: "No, no, we're practicing, we're going to reef."

Italian helmsman to deaf partner: "Quick, put on life jacket. We're going to hit the reef in big storm."

Charlie: "NO! Do not put on life jackets. We're just practicing."

Italian student: "You crazy! Not put on life jackets?! We all going to die in big storm on reef."

Charlie: "Yes, in a real situation we'd all have on life jackets. Now we're just PRACTICING."

Charlie was starting to lose it. Then he remembered the latest memo to come down from the head office, 'The most important attribute of a good instructor is patience.'

On the last day they received their certificates of competence and Charlie waited for his customary gratuity.

Italian student: "Here, please. Take all these left over groceries." He pointed to a soggy mass in the bottom of the fridge. "Thank you so much. You were wonderful." Charlie smiled politely.

Sailing with Charlie

Charlie is a most astute sailing instructor and when he found out about the 'A to Z of the Sea it became his bible. He now recommends it to all his sailing students and reportedly they have all benefited greatly.

Here are some more excerpts from this erudite book:

Clew: When Chinese press gangs shanghaied an innocent young man from a waterfront tavern for shipboard duty they would exclaim, "See that ship…You will be one of her clew!"

Cocked Hat: Erudite trigonometric shape that tells you where you might be. Derives from three lines of position from assumed known points.

Collision: When two vessels strike each other at sea. Usually collisions happen as a result of negligence since there are stringent rules to avoid such unpleasant happenings. Unfortunately many amateur mariners who take to the water are unaware of the rules. If it becomes obvious that such an amateur is approaching the D.A.W.N. rule should apply…Don't Argue With Nincompoops.

Compass: Provides some help for getting from A to B when out of sight of land. For those about to traverse the Bermuda Triangle, don't read any books about the Bermuda Triangle.

Container Ship: A huge vessel that transports large boxes of goods. No problem about deciding who has right of way. They always have right of way.

Cruise: This burgeoning vacation experience, "a cruise" incorporates a vast horizontal apartment block situated on an equally big floating structure with one pointy end: the bow. These ugly creations can accommodate hordes of tourists. On board sometimes thousands of people are fed and fattened by upwards of seven meals per day, herded around on mediocre day trips (often on large cattlemarans) and encouraged to lose money in casinos at night. Most seem to like it.

More Fantastic Bars

Abe's By The Sea

Located at Little Harbour Abe's is famous for seafood dinners especially lobster. The bar is always open as long as someone's around.

Harris' Place

Located next to Sidney's Harris' is famous for his "all you can eat" lobster dinners on Monday nights. Ice is available here along with some groceries.

Ali Baba's

Ali Baba's is right next to Jost van Dyke's administration building in Great Harbour. You can sit and wriggle your toes in the sand whilst enjoying a tropical cocktail and the restaurant offers a good selection of fish and island style dishes.

Rudy's

Rudy's is a combination, superette, bar, restaurant, and party venue at the western end of Great Harbour. Rudy sometimes plays his guitar for special parties like those that come in from the Flying Cloud, a charter "head boat." Rudy is a fisherman so fresh fish and lobster are nearly always available.

Gertrude's Bar

Gertrude's is right next to the Soggy Dollar Bar in White Bay and a large selection of lounge chairs on the sand are waiting for you and your tropical cocktail.

De Wedding

Located at the western end of Cane Garden Bay: the quiet end. It has its own tyre swing.

Clem's by the Sea

Clem used to be a bartender at the pub years ago and he really knows his drinks. Not only that but he plays steel pan music so prepare to be entertained. His bar and restaurant are located in Carrot Bay across from the park. The restaurant specializes in local dishes like goat water, fish and fungi and conch.

Bing's Drop Inn Bar

Bing's, at East End village, is popular as a late night venue. Dancing goes on till late and bar meals can be had.

Top of the Baths

The Top of the Baths is at an absolutely outstanding location with a panoramic view of the out islands and Tortola. Yachties can walk up the trail from The Baths. There's an interesting fresh water pool here and the bar/restaurant, adjacent to a small shopping complex, serves up burgers, fish and chips, sandwiches, salads and other lunchtime specials.

The Dog and Dolphin

The Dog and Dolphin is a "swim up bar" at Nail Bay, a retirement and rental home community, at Virgin Gorda's northwestern end. There are fantastic views overlooking The Dog Islands and Tortola. You can enjoy the Jacuzzi while waiting for your island style meal. Open for lunch and dinner.

The Poor Man's Bar

Right on the beach at the famous Baths. Cold beer, drinks and sandwiches are available.

Pancho's

Pancho's is in Gun Creek, at the end of the road. Real island style food available here and you can play pool while you're waiting.

The Big Banana

The Big Banana is right next to Rhymer's at Cane Garden Bay. They serve breakfast, lunch and dinner and prices are reasonable. There is entertainment on some nights. In the same premises are a gift shop and an ice cream stand.

Stanley's

Some thirty-five years ago Stanley's emerged as the first beach bar in Cane Garden Bay. The restaurant became famous for lobster dinners, pina coladas and the steel pan band that played after dinner. It was the blueprint for many to follow. Outside the bar, tied to a tall overhanging palm tree, was a tire swing. Stanley's and the tire swing were featured on thousands of postcards and calendars and became the quintessential trademark of the British Virgin Islands. It's still there and many still stop by on a trip down memory lane.

Bomba's Shack

Bomba's achieved world fame when it was featured in the Sport's Illustrated Swimsuit Edition some years back. Bomba's famous full moon parties are legendary with mushroom tea being served at midnight.

Smuggler's Cove

Smuggler's Cove is the furthest beach to the west on Tortola's north shore. Its close proximity to St. Thomas and St. John is undoubtedly responsible for its name, coupled with its remoteness from the authorities. It has a pretty, crescent-shaped and palm-lined, sandy beach and a coral reef not far offshore for snorkeling. The beach bar is tucked behind the palms.

Anegada Reef Hotel
Free Drink: Famous Rum Smoothie

Bananakeet Café
Free Drink: Happy hour cocktail

Bat Cave
Free: A Sample of each of our Specialty Drinks

The Bath and Turtle
Free Drink: Special of the Day (2 for 1)

The Big Bamboo
Free Drink: Bamboo Teaser (2 for 1)

The Bitter End
Free Drink: Painkiller (2 for 1)

Castaways
Free Drink: Island Eater (Peppermint Schnapps and Bailey's Irish Cream)

Corsairs
Free Drink: Beer or Well Drink (2 for 1)

The Cow Wreck

Cow Wreck
Free: Shuttle bus to restaurant with dinner reservation

Cybercafe
Free Drink: 2 for 1 "Turbokiller"

D' Best Cup
Trellis Bay

D' Best Cup
Free Coffee: Refill of their tasty regular blend

Emile's
Free Drink: 2 for 1 Strawberry Margarita

Fat Hog Bob's
Free Drink: Hogwash (Rum with tropical juices)

Fat Virgin Café
Free Drink: Rum Punch

Foxy's
Free Drink:
"Born 'ere draft beer"

Foxy's Taboo
Free Drink: Born 'ere Beer

Ivan's
Local
Flavor

Ivan's Local Flavor
Honor Bar
Help Yourself!

The Jolly Roger
Free Drink: Rum Punch
(2 for 1)

Jumbies at Leverick Bay
Free Drink:
Bushwacker or Painkiller

Kong Ming
Free Appetiser: Fried
Wantons: Chicken in Crispy
Pastry (one portion/table)

The Last Resort
Free Drink: Island Moose

Le Cabanon
Free: Rum Punch

De Loose Mongoose
Free Drink: Tropical Noseeum

The Mine Shaft
Free Drink: Cave In

Myett's
Free: Bottle of wine with dinner (one per table)

Neptune's Treasure
Free: Bottle of wine with dinner (one per table)

One Love
Free Drink: Bushwacker (2 for 1)

Peg Leg's Landing
Free: Drink with dinner